TEA SHOP WALKS
IN THE
LAKE DISTRICT

Jean Patefield

Published by Sigma Leisure – an imprint of
Sigma Press, 1 South Oak Lane, Wilmslow, Cheshire SK9 6AR, England.

British Library Cataloguing in Publication Data
A CIP record for this book is available from the British Library.

ISBN: 1-85058-417-6

Typesetting and Design by: Sigma Press, Wilmslow, Cheshire.

Cover photograph: Elterwater and The Langdales (Jean Patefield)

Maps and photographs: the author

Printed by: MFP Design & Print

Disclaimer: the information in this book is given in good faith and is believed to be correct at the time of publication. No responsibility is accepted by either the author or publisher for errors or omissions, or for any loss or injury howsoever caused. Only you can judge your own fitness, competence and experience.

Contents

Summary of Walks

WALK	LOCATION	DISTANCE	TEASHOP	DESCRIPTION
1	Lakeside	2 miles	Cafe at steamer pier and station.	Quiet woods and fields. One climb. Train ride.
2	Grizedale	5½ miles	Forest visitor centre.	Forest walk. Two climbs. Interesting forest sculptures.
3	The Sawreys	4 miles	Traditional.	Easy walk. One climb. Beatrix Potter country.
4	Views of Windermere	7 miles	Traditional - wide choice in Bowness	Surprisingly quiet. Two climbs. Visits three viewpoints.
5	Ravenglass	3½ miles	Muncaster Castle - no charge to call at tea shop	The Lake District's seaside. Two climbs. Roman remains.
6	Tarn Hows and Coniston	6 miles	Traditional - wide choice in Coniston	Woods and fields, waterfall and Tarn Hows. Two climbs.
7	Hawkshead	6 miles	Traditional - wide choice in Hawkshead	Woods and fields. Two climbs. Can be muddy.
8	Jenkin Grag and Waterhead	3 miles	Traditional - wide choice in Waterhead	Climb through woods to viewpoint. Roman remains.
9	Little Langdale	6 miles	Pub	Fell walk, needs clear weather. Two climbs.

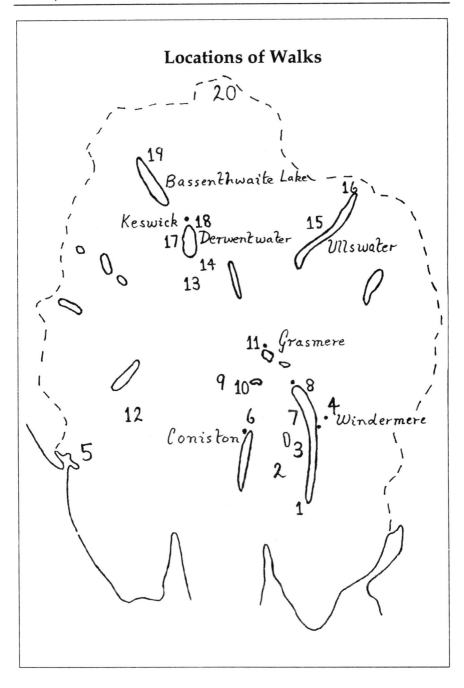

Key to symbols used on sketch maps

Path on route	$- - \rightarrow$
Path not on route	$\cdot \; \cdot \; \cdot$
Road	
River	
Lake	
Church	
Tea Shop	
Summit	$\triangle$
Point in text	$\left(4\right)$
Car Park	$\square$
Building referred to in text	

THE LAKE DISTRICT

The Lake District is England's best-loved walking area. It has cast its spell over visitors since the earliest days of tourism over two hundred years ago. Crammed into this blessed corner of North West England is much that represents the best of British landscape. Rugged mountains soar skywards. In fact, they are modest in scale but by some trick of scale give every impression of brooding magnificence as they are mirrored in the serene lakes beneath. Tiny tarns lie like jewels among the hills just waiting to be discovered while, between the hills, are long dales of peaceful pasture with woods and rivers in which nestle ancient towns and delightful villages.

Thousands escape to its freedom and beauty every year and yet there are many quiet corners where its peace can be enjoyed away from the crowds. It exerts its special charm at all times of the year and is never the same as the light and weather change so markedly with the seasons. No corner of England has attracted so many writers and artists and it has inspired some of the best-loved poetry and prose.

To the visitor, the mountains seem unchanging, their shapes as recognizable as the faces of well-loved friends. Taking a longer perspective, that is an illusion caused by our short life span compared with the immensity of geological time. At different periods in the Earth's history, the area we know as one of mountains and lakes was once at the bottom of the sea, blasted by volcanos, made into an arid wind-blown desert and then buried beneath thousands of feet of ice. All of these circumstances have contributed to the landscape we see today.

The Lake District today consists of three main types of rock surrounded by a rim of a fourth type. Each rock contributes its own distinctive landscape. (Of course, this statement is an oversimplification of what is a complex area geologically and for a more complete account, see the Sigma Leisure publication 'Lakeland Rocky Rambles' by Bryan Lynas.)

The oldest rocks are the Skiddaw slates in the north. They were formed from the mud and silt that accumulated on the bed of a vast ocean about 500 million years ago. Since then they have been covered by later deposits and uncovered and worn away by the erosive forces of water, wind and ice. They weather quite evenly and so they produced the rounded, smooth hills such as Saddleback and Skiddaw, towering above Keswick, from which they get their name.

The dramatic crags of central Lakeland such as Scafell and the Langdales originated in volcanoes which thrust through the sea bed with explosive violence, scattering fragments of rock far and wide. Lava flowed out and in periods of violent eruption vast quantities of dust were ejected which later consolidated to form volcanic ash and breccia. The volcanic cones built up above the sea bed and again, vast layers of rock accumulated which are now known as the Borrowdale Volcanic series.

The third type of rock, the Silurian slates, gives a more gentle and pastoral landscape because it is more easily eroded and forms a deeper, more fertile soil. It is found in the South around Windermere and extends towards Kendal. It too was laid down at the bottom of the sea from mud and silt particles formed from the erosion of ancient mountains.

Since these three categories of rock were formed, the rock strata have been subject to stupendous physical forces: thrown up into folds by the colliding of continents and worn down by water, wind and ice. At one time, during the Carboniferous period some 300 million years ago, the land which is now the Lake District was covered by a warm, clear sea in which corals and other sea life flourished. Thick layers of limestone were formed. The sea was never very deep and eventually it filled up completely and was colonised by a marshy forest of huge ferns. From these, the coal measures of the Whitehaven – Maryport coal field were formed and the fire clays under most of the seams are the remains of the soil in which this forest once grew. Eventually, this limestone was eroded away and now remains as a rim around the Lake District.

The single most important influence forming the area we know today was ice. Over a million years ago the climate began to get colder and more snow fell than the sun could melt in the summer: the last great Ice Age had begun. Gradually it got thicker and thicker until only the tips of the highest mountains peeped through. Great glaciers ground their way down the valleys, carrying debris with them. Sometimes the climate became a bit warmer and the ice loosened its grip for a while only to readvance and cover the land again.

The ice, loaded with rock debris, scoured the land. Valleys were deepened and straightened as jutting spurs were eroded. The shape of the valleys altered from the typical 'V' formed by water erosion to a smoother 'U' shape. Side valleys were left as hanging valleys by this deepening effect on the main valley. Rocks at the bottom of the valley were scratched by fragments of ice carried along by the glacier and these can still be seen today.

Blelham Tarn, seen on Walk 7

Some ten to twenty thousand years ago the ice began to melt, hopefully for the last time – though we have no assurance that there will not be a fresh advance: we may just be in a warm interglacial period, such as there has been before. As the ice melted, masses of clay and debris were dumped and choked the natural outlets from the valleys. Thus many of the deepened valleys were dammed and the lakes were formed, fanning out like the spokes of a wheel from a central hub.

The lakes are the essential counterpoint to the mountains. The water which fills them and provides the music of the valleys as streams tumble over rocks was once rain. It is an inescapable fact of life that as moist air from the Atlantic rises to cross the land it cools and the water vapour condenses out and falls as rain. The Lake District does not have more rainy days than, say, London but Lake District rain can be prolonged and peculiarly wetting in its consistency. The wise walker goes prepared. Remember that William Wordsworth died of a cold caught, it is said, by walking in the rain without a hat!

The landscape we see today is not the product of geological forces and weather alone. Man may have visited the area before the last Ice Age but, if so, left no record. Since returning as the ice retreated human beings have had as much impact on what we see as the ice did. Left to Nature, all but the highest hills would be covered by a thick cloak of forest. Oak mixed with other trees would cover the lower slopes and pine and birch scrub would grow on the higher hills, so only the tops of the highest peaks would poke out above a sea of forest. Similarly the valleys such as Borrowdale, Langdale and Newlands would be impassable with alder swamp. Over the centuries the landscape has been moulded to fit human purposes so what we admire today is as much the creation of man as nature.

The transformation of the landscape began about 5000 years ago when human beings started to take control of the environment, almost unnoticeably at first but with ever increasing power that led inexorably to the man-made landscape we see today. Not only could stone axes cut down the forest, but animals such as pigs and goats grazing in the forest nibbled away the young shoots and prevented the forest regenerating. Today there is virtually none of the original forest cover left, though the Keskadale oaks in Newlands valley may be a remnant.

Much of the clearance of the primeval forest happened during the time after the Norman Conquest when the area was mainly dominated by the great abbeys such as Furness. The monks developed the wool trade by opening up the fells as sheep walks. As the soil was exposed it became impoverished by the leaching of minerals by the rain and bracken and matt grass took over more and more. Animals which once roamed the area such as boar, wolves and golden eagles were driven from the land. The miles of dry stone walls now seem almost part of the natural landscape but they were mainly built in the latter half of the eighteenth century and the first half of the nineteenth century when labour was cheap. Population pressures drove farming into ever more remote and inaccessible areas.

The amount of woodland has increased due to reafforestation and is now about ten per cent. About half is native broadleaved woodland, while the rest is conifer plantations. 5000 acres of the broadleaved woodland is protected by being owned by the National Trust and the Park Authority owns over a thousand acres more. Some of the woods are Sites of Special Scientific Interest because of their lichens, mosses and liverworts. The woods still harbour red squirrels and are home to many red deer, a rare sight for noisy human visitors.

Teals, tufted ducks, merganser, goosander mallard and mute swans breed here and are joined in winter by many visitors such as goldeneye and widgeon. Ravens and peregrine falcons swoop over the fells and crags and a native bird, the golden eagle, has recently returned with one pair breeding successfully for several years.

Though today we do not think of it as such, the area has long been an industrial one. The value of the volcanic stone in the centre of the Lake District was recognised 5000 years ago and used to make stone axes which were exported to Ireland and Brittany as well as other parts of Britain. Another valuable product torn from the heart of the area is slate, used by the Romans to roof their buildings and still quarried today. Unlike more fertile areas, the Romans seem to have come here more as an army of occupation than to settle. What attracted them was the copper and lead in the rocks and the mining of these was an important local industry until quite recent times. In the reign of Queen Elizabeth I, German miners were brought to the Lake District to improve the efficiency of mining. The Moot Hall in Keswick was rebuilt in 1571 as the Queen's receiving house for copper. Smelting was carried out at Brigham by the river Greta and the works were considered the finest of their kind in Europe in their day.

The beauty and grandeur of the Lakes has inspired generations of artists and writers. William Wordsworth was the quintessential poet of place and several of the walks in this book visit the localities associated with him. He attracted many leading literary contemporaries, most notably Samuel Taylor Coleridge and Robert Southey. The friends and colleagues who visited Wordsworth were the vanguard of the army of tourists who have been drawn to the region since the eighteenth century. Wordsworth wrote his famous 'Guide to the Lakes' but regretted the invasion of tourists and campaigned against the coming of the railway which opened up the area to the less leisured and less wealthy (though he apparently owned shares in the railway company).

Wordsworth wrote his guide in 1835 but he was not the first and has been followed by countless others. One of the most interesting was Harriet Martineau whose 'Complete Guide to the English Lakes' was published in 1855. It is a racy and idiosyncratic mixture of fact, legend, hearsay and political comment. She was born in Norwich in 1802 and was plain, almost deaf and subject to periods of ill health. Not surprisingly, she did not have the sweetest of tempers. When her father died in 1825 she had to make a living in a world where education and opportunities for women were severely restricted. She achieved this with her needle and her pen and achieved success as a journalist and commentator. In 1846 she had a house built near Ambleside and was visited by many Establishment figures of the day despite her stern manner and Radical views.

Not all the writers inspired by the Lake District have been moved to great poetry. Arthur Ransome based his children's classics, of which 'Swallows and Amazons' is the most famous, in Lakeland.

Beatrix Potter was inspired by family holidays in the Lakes and later moved there, married and as Mrs William Heelis took up sheep farming. She used the money that she made to buy tracts of land which she gave to the National Trust.

The modern author who has done most to present the Lake District to a wide audience is Alfred Wainwright. He was born in Blackburn in 1907 and worked in local government. He fell in love with the area during walking trips as a young man and in 1941 he moved to Kendal where he eventually became Borough Treasurer. His seven 'Pictorial Guides to the Lakeland Fells' were compiled between 1952 and 1966 and his evocative descriptions, distinctive drawings and acerbic asides have made them the indispensable companions of all fellwalkers.

The Lake District is so small and vulnerable that it could easily be loved to death. Some sort of protection and management is vital to conserve what Wordsworth referred to as 'a sort of national property'. Two important, though very different, bodies are the National Trust and the National Park.

The National Trust was founded by three Victorians of energy and enthusiasm. One was Canon Harwicke Rawnsley who was the vicar of Crosthwaite near Keswick as well as being a poet, athlete, traveller and historian. A parishioner told him in 1890 that he had been forced to buy a piece of land from a neighbour to prevent some fine trees being felled. Rawnsley took the idea of protection by purchase and with Octavia Hill and Robert Hunter, the National Trust was launched in 1895. It aims to acquire land and property of scenic beauty or historical interest and under the National Trust Act of 1907 it can declare its property 'inalienable'. This means that it cannot be sold or mortgaged and later legislation gave it the right to appeal to Parliament against compulsory purchase orders.

Today the National Trust – which is not a government department or quango but a charity depending on its millions of members for support – is the largest landowner in the Lake District. Much of its property was acquired by gift. For example, Beatrix Potter gave 4000 acres including fourteen farms. The work of the National Trust has enabled traditional farming practices to continue and so conserved the well-loved landscape. One advantage of the National Trust from the point of view of the visitor is that its properties are open to the public subject only to the needs of farming, forestry and the conservation of wildlife.

The first National Park in the world was Yellowstone in the USA, created in 1872 to protect that magnificent area of wilderness from development. In England, by the time the idea caught on, there was no wilderness left. Thus, in an English context, the term National Parks is something of a misnomer since they are neither National nor parks! Unlike the USA for example, the land is not owned by the nation but by private individuals or bodies such as the National Trust, and within the bounds are towns and villages. Agriculture and industry continue. It is more of a planning concept to give special protection to areas of outstanding landscape value.

The Lake District is the largest of the National Parks in England and Wales and the Act, delayed by the War, which brought them into being was passed in 1949, seventy-seven years after the establishment of Yellowstone. The National Park Authority has planning control, provides information and ranger services and maintains footpaths. It also owns tracts of commonland, woods and some of the lakes. The National Park works closely with the National Trust and other large landowners to provide a degree of protection and public access unrivalled elsewhere in England.

Tea shops

Tea is often said to be the best meal to eat out in England: scones with cream and strawberry jam, delicious home-made cakes, toasted tea cakes dripping with butter in winter, delicate cucumber sandwiches in summer – all washed down with the cup that cheers! Bad for the figure maybe, but the walking will see to that.

The best tea shops offer a range of cakes, all home-made and including fruit cake as well as scones and other temptations. Cream teas should, of course, feature clotted cream. Tea pots should be capacious and pour properly. Ideally, there should be an attractive garden where tea can be taken outside in summer. Many of the tea shops visited on these walks fulfil all these criteria admirably.

Tea shops are not scattered evenly through the Lake District. In some tourist honeypots such as Hawkshead or Grasmere the visitor is spoilt for choice. In such cases the tea shop which, in the author's opinion, most closely fulfils the criteria set out above is recommended but should that not appeal there are others to choose from. In other places there is Hobson's choice and therefore a few of the tea shops visited on the walks in this book are in unusual places such as gardens and stately homes. However, that in itself adds interest to the walk and they all offer a good tea part way round an attractive walk.

The opening times and telephone number of each tea shop is given. Many are rather vague about when they open out of season: it seems to depend on weather and mood. If you are planning a walk on a November Tuesday, for example, a call to check that tea will actually be available that day is a wise precaution.

The walks

The twenty walks in this book are all between 2 and 8 miles and should be within the capacity of the average person. They are intended to take the walker through some of the loveliest scenery in England at a gentle pace with plenty of time to stop and stare, to savour the beauty and interest all around. A dedicated yomper and stomper could probably knock off the whole book in a single weekend but in doing so they would have missed the point and seen nothing. To fully appreciate the countryside it is necessary to go slowly with your eyes and ears open.

Some of the walks stick to the valleys and are fairly level. Others venture into the hills and so involve some climbing. However, this presents no problem to the sensible walker who has three uphill gears – slowly, very slowly and admiring the view. None of the walks in this book are inherently hazardous but sensible care should be taken. A lot of the falls which do happen are due to unsuitable footwear, particularly smooth soles since steep grass can be as slippery as the more obviously hazardous wet, smooth rock. Proper walking shoes or boots also give some protection to the ankle. It is also essential to look where you are putting your feet to avoid tripping up. Wainwright said that he never had a serious fall in all his years and thousands of miles of walking because he always looked where he put his feet and he stopped if he wanted to admire the scenery.

All the routes are on public rights of way, permissive paths or open fell and have been carefully checked but, of course, in the countryside things do change; a gate is replaced by a stile or a wood is extended. In the Lake District the paths are often (but not always) well used and well maintained so the routes are easy to follow.

Each walk is illustrated by a map and they are all circular. An Ordnance Survey map is useful as well, especially for identifying the main features of views. There are several from which to choose so no specific recommendations are made. The Lake District is covered by Landranger 1:50000 (1¼ inches to 1 mile) series sheets 89, 90 91, 96 and 97 and there is also a Tourist Map showing most of the National Park on a single sheet at 1 inch to the mile. The same area is also covered on four 1:25000 (2½ inches to 1 mile) maps in the Outdoor Leisure Series. These do not include the peripheral areas which are covered by the standard Pathfinder 1:25000 maps.

The walks are designed so that, starting where suggested, the teashop is reached in the second half so a really good appetite for tea can be worked up. The starting point of some walks can be reached easily by public transport. Most of the others can be reached by public transport if the route is modified slightly to start from a different place.

1. Lakeside

Route:	This is an attractive short walk through woods and fields which can be combined with a ride on a steam train. It is ideal for children or a showery day when the walk can be done in a quick dash between raindrops. It is on quiet paths somewhat off the beaten track.
Teashop:	The Station Cafe at Lakeside above the station has extensive views over Windermere and offers a good selection of cakes as well as full meals. It is open all day in the summer.
Tel:	015395 31188
Distance:	2 miles
How to get there:	The walk described here starts at Newby Bridge Halt (SD 366864) on the Lakeside and Haverthwaite Railway. The parking near Newby Bridge Halt is rather limited so the suggested plan is to take the train from Haverthwaite Station, where there is a large car park, get out at Newby Bridge Halt, walk to Lakeside and then catch the train back to Haverthwaite. Steam trains run daily at Easter and from the end of April to the end of October and the times can be confirmed by telephoning Haverthwaite Station (015395 31594). Haverthwaite Station is on the A590 2 miles west of Newby Bridge.
Start:	Haverthwaite Station. SD 350842

1. Book a return ticket to Lakeside and get out at Newby Bridge Halt. Go to the road and turn left to the road junction at the Swan Hotel.

There is a path parallel with the road on the bank of the River Leven for most of this. Turn left and walk over the railway bridge.

This railway was built as part of the Ulverston to Lakeside line. It was closed in the mid-1960s and reopened in 1973 by the Lakeside and Haverthwaite Railway Co. Ltd. which is supported by the Lakeside Railway Society. The line runs for $3\frac{1}{2}$ miles of lovely scenery by the River Leven. The trains are usually hauled by steam locomotives. The sheds are at Haverthwaite and there are several locomotives to be seen, lovingly restored and maintained by enthusiasts.

Lakeside and Haverthwaite railway

2. Immediately after the bridge, turn left on a track. Ignore a path on the right after 50 yards and continue on the track between buildings to a gate and shortly after bear left at a fork. Just over the brow of the hill go through a gap in a wall and continue across a crossing path to reach a stile over a wall into a field.

3. The path is not visible on the ground but goes more or less across the field to a squeeze stile at the far side. The well-nourished walker may find it easier to go a few feet right to a gap in the wall. Go slightly right across the second field to a ladder stile over the wall and then straight ahead across the third field to yet another stile. Finsthwaite Church now comes into view. Make straight for it across the fourth field to a gate onto a lane.

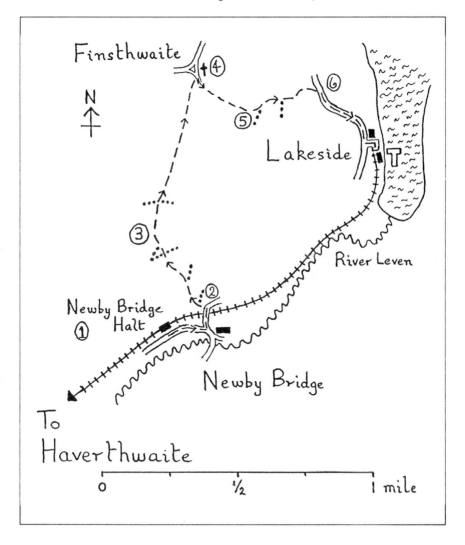

In Finsthwaite churchyard, on the south side of the church, is the grave of Clementina Johannes Sobieska Douglas. She is said to have been the illegitimate daughter of Bonnie Prince Charlie but there is no record of his having visited her when he stayed in Kendal. Inside the church is a communion cup made from a shell and a cross made from a plank that was part of a pontoon bridge over the River Piave in Italy. They were made for a former vicar who had been stationed in Northern Italy towards the end of the First World War.

4. Turn right. After about 100 yards the surfaced lane ends. Go through a gate and continue in the same direction across two fields to a stile into a wood.

5. Follow the clear path through the wood ignoring two paths on the right.

6. At the road, turn right for about a quarter of a mile and then turn left immediately after the Lakeside Hotel to the shore of Windermere. The teashop is above the station on the right. After tea, catch the train back to Haverthwaite.

The teashop has excellent views up Windermere which is the largest lake in England being over 10½ miles long and more than a mile wide at its widest point. It was gouged out in the Ice Age by glaciers moving down from the fells to the north. Today, after thousands of years of filling by silt washed down from the surrounding hills, it is still over 200 feet deep in places.

The lake has always been one of the busiest and people have enjoyed cruises on the lake since the first public vessel was launched in 1845. This was *The Lady of the Lake* which was a schooner-rigged paddle steamer and it carried 5000 passengers in its first season. There were vociferous complaints from the locals who complained that it destroyed the peace of the lake. Today, three vessels cruise from Lakeside at the southern end of the lake to Waterhead at the northern end. They are *Teal* and *Swan* built by Vickers Armstrong of Barrow in 1936 and 1938 respectively, and the oldest ship *Tern* built by Forrests of Wyvenhoe in 1891. The latter was used as a training ship in World War II and renamed *HMS Undine*. A fourth ship, *Swift*, now houses an exhibition about the Campbells (see Walk 6, page 45).

The west bank of Windermere attracted many wealthy industrialists who built elegant mansions along its banks. These are now mainly converted into hotels and centres such as the National Park Centre at Brockholes. Their presence restricts access to the lake and gives some idea of what the Lakes might have been like without conservation bodies such as the National Trust.

One such industrialist was Henry William Schneider who bought the building which is now the Belsfield Hotel at Bowness. He was chairman of Barrow Steelworks and Shipyard and every morning he cruised down the lake in his steam launch *Esperance* while eating his breakfast. At Lakeside he joined his personal coach on the train to Barrow. He was never in any danger of missing the train as he owned the railway too. *Esperance* is now in the Windermere Steam Boat Museum.

2. *Grizedale*

Route:	This is an interesting walk through Grizedale Forest. It is on well-defined paths and tracks through the forest and there are some fine views and beautiful woodland scenery. It is perhaps particularly suitable for inclement weather as much of the walk is on forestry tracks which are well-constructed and the trees provide some protection.
Teashop:	The tea room at Grizedale Forest Visitor Centre offers an excellent range of delicious cakes. It is open during the summer every day from 10.00am until 5.00pm and also at the weekend in winter.
Tel:	01229 860011
Distance:	5½ miles
How to get there:	From Hawkshead, go through Grizedale and Satterthwaite and cross the bridge over Grizedale Beck. After a further 150 yards there is a parking space on the right.
Start:	Parking space 400 yards south of Satterthwaite. SD 336919

1. From the parking space turn left along the road over the bridge into Satterthwaite. Continue through the village past the church.

Satterthwaite gets its name from the Old Norse: a 'saetre' was a summer farm and 'thwaite' means a clearing so the name means 'summer farm in a clearing'. It probably then belonged to the Viking Rolf who lived further down the valley at Rusland.

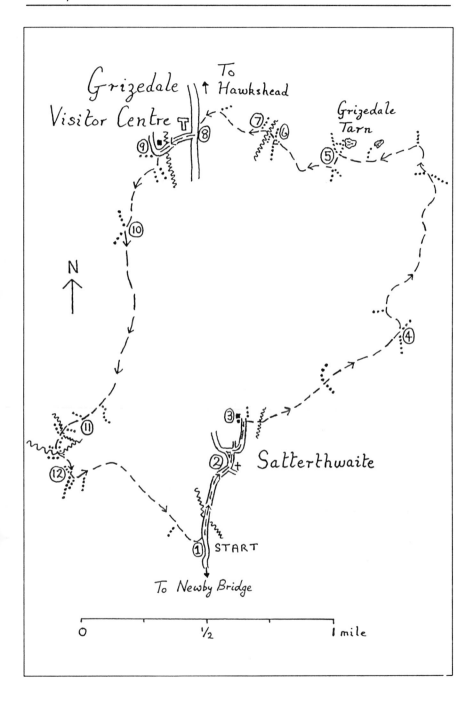

2. As the main road bears left, continue ahead on a minor road and then turn right at the T-junction on a lane which climbs up out of the village to a house.

3. Opposite the first house, turn right on a rising path signed as a bridleway to Dale Park. Stay on this well-defined path as it crosses a stream and a forestry track.

Grizedale was originally covered by mixed oak woods, as were all the valleys in Lakeland, but these were all cut down for charcoal to use in the smelting of iron. There are several 'bloomeries' where haematite was smelted in the valley. By the eighteenth century the woods had been over exploited and could no longer support the industry. The Grizedale estate then started to plant conifers to use as pit props and this policy was continued by the Forestry Commission when it acquired the estate in 1936. Grizedale Forest is some 4200 acres between Estwaite and Coniston Water.

The Forestry Commission was set up in 1919 to create a strategic reserve of timber and conifers are very quick growing in the warm(!), wet British climate. Some broadleaved trees remain particularly in the valley bottom where they were planted as ornamental trees round Grizedale Hall.

The value of forests for recreation has been realised in more recent years as woods can absorb a lot of people without losing a sense of remoteness. Grizedale was one of the first forests to be opened up to the public and many trails of different types have been created to help the public enjoy the forest. The forest also has abundant wild life, especially red and roe deer, but the shy creatures are not likely to be seen by noisy people.

4. At a second forestry track turn left. Continue on this track for about a mile until you see a tarn on the right. Ignore a forestry track on the right after about $^3/_4$ mile as the main track bends left.

As you go round this walk, you will come across some startling structures. In 1977 a scheme was launched to encourage sculptors to use the forest as an inspiration and working environment. There are now some fifty scattered around the forest and more information about them is available from the Visitor Centre.

The Old Man of The Forest

5. Turn left on a forestry track. (The path on the right leads to Grizedale Tarn which is a pleasant place to linger.) After 125 yards turn right on a clear path. The path branches just before it reaches a forest track. Take the left branch which goes down some steps onto the track.

6. Turn right for 30 yards and then turn left on a path which goes down into a dip, across a stream and up the other side to a stile into a field.

7. The path is not very obvious on the ground but goes ahead with first a wall and then a wire fence on the left to a wooden gate where it joins a larger path. There is an interestingly designed and well-placed seat here. Turn left down to the road. The tea shop is in the buildings across the road.

The Visitor Centre and forest offices are housed in what were once the outbuildings of Grizedale Hall with some recent additions. Grizedale Hall was demolished after serving as a prisoner of war camp during the Second World War. The Visitor Centre offers many facilities including, of course, the excellent tea shop.

The Theatre in the Forest was opened in 1970 and musicians of national and international repute appear regularly. A redundant saw mill has been made into the Gallery in the Forest and there are regular exhibitions. Through the shop is an interesting display about the history and management of the forest. There is also a children's playground.

8. Return to the road and turn right. After 50 yards turn right on a side road.

9. Immediately after a farm on the right as the road bends right, turn left on a track over a cattle grid. Ignore paths on the left and continue up to a gate.

10. Through the gate turn left on a cross track. Follow this track as it

more or less contours along the hill side, ignoring all side paths and tracks.

11. After about three-quarters of a mile, the track divides. Take the left branch. Stay on the same track across two streams and as it bends left then right.

At the second stream it is well worth going a few yards upstream, to the right, to one of the sculptures. It is an elaborately carved water wheel with a lever to direct the stream of water onto the wheel.

12. As the track climbs away from the second stream watch for a path on the right, marked by a green-topped post. Take a similarly marked path on the left 20 yards further on. After 60 yards turn left on a broad crossing track. This leads gently downhill to the parking place where the walk started. There are some fine views across the forest to the left and, at the time of writing, a seat well-placed to appreciate them.

3. The Sawreys

Route:	This is an easy and delightful walk round Beatrix Potter country. There is a mile along a road but this is on a quiet lane which contours along the hillside and has attractive views of Grizedale Forest. Earlier in the walk there are extensive views across Esthwaite Water.
Teashop:	Buckle Yeat in Near Sawrey is a charming tea shop and guest house in one of the buildings which appears in several Beatrix Potter books. The teapots are pleasingly capacious and the toasted teacakes particularly good. There is a garden at the back. It is open when Hill Top, Beatrix Potter's house in Near Sawrey, is open which is Easter to October except Thursday and Friday.
Tel:	015394 36446
Distance:	4 miles
How to get there:	The walk starts in Far Sawrey which is on the B5285 between Hawkshead and the ferry to Bowness. Coming from Hawkshead, Far Sawrey is the second village you come to, whereas coming from the ferry it is the first village.
Start:	The walk starts at the telephone box in Far Sawrey. SD 379954

1. From the telephone box walk along the road past the Sawrey Hotel and take the first road on the right. 100 yards after a gate and cattle grid bear left on an unsurfaced track. A track from Near Sawrey joins on the left. Continue ahead (signed to Claife Heights) for about a quarter of a mile ignoring side tracks.

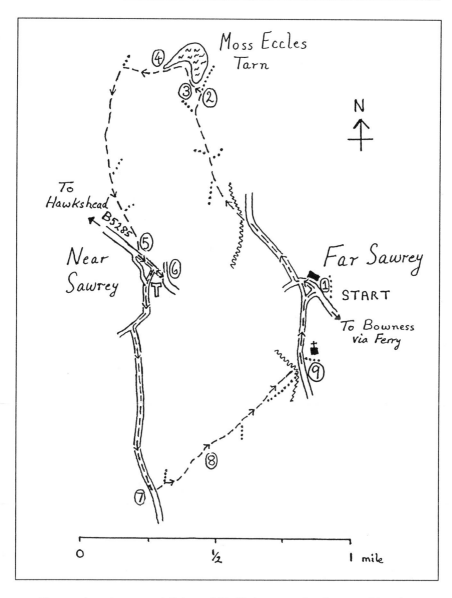

The curiously-named Crier of Claife bar at the Sawrey Hotel
gets its name from a ghost which was reputed to haunt the
Claife Heights above the village. The ferry across Windermere
used to be operated by one man and intending passengers from

the other shore had to shout for him. Legend has it that a
monk from Furness Abbey who took a particular interest in
fallen women (!) fell for one but was rejected. He went mad and
his ghost haunted the heights crying out. One night the ferry
man went out in response to his cries and returned next
morning with white hair and never spoke again before he died a
few days later. For this reason, the ferry only ran in daylight
hours as no sensible ferry man would be tempted away from a
warm and comfortable fireside to risk the cold and dark . . . and
ghosts. The ghost is supposed to have been exorcised and
confined to Claife Quarry.

2. Immediately after a gate across the main track, the wall on the left
   bears away from the track. Leave the track at this point and walk
   left by the wall up a rise to Moss Eccles tarn.

   Moss Eccles tarn appears in one of Beatrix Potter's books –
   Jeremy Fisher. It is a delightful tarn which has water lilies in
   season. It has many inviting spots in which to linger.

3. Take the permissive path to the left of the tarn to a stile.

4. Over the stile, the path is not visible on the ground. Bear half right
   to eventually come to a track. Turn left and follow the track downhill
   with a wall on the right to a road.

   The lake seen below is Esthwaite Water, appreciated by
   Wordsworth when he was a pupil at Hawkshead Grammar
   School:

   > . . . My morning walks were early;
   > oft before the hours of school
   > I travelled round our little lake,
   > Five mile of pleasant wandering.
   > Happy time!

   Lying on soft, easily eroded rock and surrounded by farm land,

Esthwaite Water is rich in nutrients and therefore supports particularly good fishing.

5. Turn left and follow the road into Near Sawrey. The tea shop is on the right and Hill Top, Beatrix Potter's home, is a little further on.

Near Sawrey has been immortalised by one of the National Trust's greatest benefactors. Beatrix Potter first came to Near Sawrey in 1896 when her parents took a house (now called Ees Wyke) for a holiday. She fell in love with the area and was eventually able to buy Hill Top. She did not live there permanently but stayed for weeks at a time and had a manager to look after the farm. At this time she was at her most prolific and wrote thirteen books. The charming illustrations were not produced from Beatrix Potter's imagination and many of the scenes can be recognised around Near Sawrey.

Buckle Yeat Tea Shop

She bought more properties in the area and married the solicitor who had acted for her in the purchases. As Mrs. William Heelis, she was less interested in writing and more interested in farming.

Hill Top is in the care of the National Trust and is open from Easter to October from 11.00am to 5.00pm. It is very small and can be rather crowded. It is rather expensive to visit unless you are a member of the National Trust.

6. Retrace your steps past the car park for Hill Top and take a minor road on the left signed to Lakeside. Ignore the road on the right and turn left at the next junction where there is a seat well-placed to enjoy the superb view.

7. After $^1/_2$ mile, take a public footpath on the left signed to Far Sawrey. Ignore a path on the left after 50 yards and follow the clear path through the wood to a stile into a field.

8. The path through the field is not very clear on the ground to begin with. It goes directly across a large field to a gate and then across a small field to a gate and stile. In the third field bear left on a track beside a wire fence. Over the stile follow the track round to the right following a line of fine oaks.

9. At a lane, turn left into Far Sawrey. When the lane forks, bear right back to the starting point.

4. Views of Windermere

Route: This walk starts at a viewpoint over Windermere, climbs to the classic view from Orrest Head, visits the lakeside town of Bowness and towards the end has an optional short detour to the second classic viewpoint of Queen Adelaide's Hill. Most of the walk is through very pretty countryside and is remarkably quiet, considering how close it is to Windermere town and Bowness. The route also passes the Steam Boat Museum on the shore of Windermere.

Teashop: There are many tea shops and cafes of all descriptions in Bowness. The one that fits in best with the theme of this walk is the Bowness Pier cafe, right on the lake front with unimpeded views across the lake. It is open from 9.00am to 5.00pm but is closed in January. A classic teashop is Hedgerow Tearoom, open every day from 10.30am to 5.00pm (5.30pm at weekends) but this is a couple of hundred yards off the main route.

Tel: Hedgerow Teashop, 015394 45002; Bowness Pier Cafe, 015394 42747

Distance: 7 miles

How to get there: From the A591 Windermere – Ambleside road, take the A592 signed to Bowness Bay and The Lake. Hammar Bank car park is about 250 yards from the junction.

Start: Hammar Bank car park. SD 406991. This is the first viewpoint and at the southern end of the car park is a plaque illustrating the main features of the view.

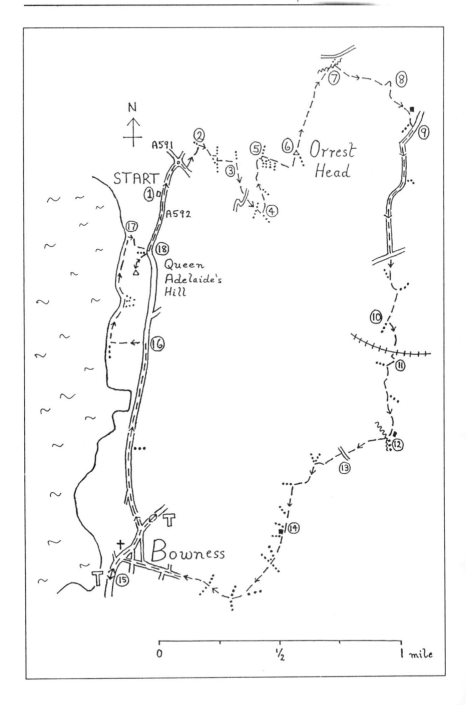

1. From the car park turn left to the roundabout. Turn right for 100 yards and then take a public footpath on the left along the drive to Wynlass Bank Stables. Cross the stream, go through a gate and then up some small steps to the right of a barn. The path is signed but the sign is presently obscured by ivy growing on the barn. The path goes over a squeeze stile in a gate, passes the exercise yard and in a few yards goes through a hidden kissing gate on the right. Follow the path between hedge and fence to a track.

2. Turn right and follow the track between houses, going through a gate across the track. Just after the entrance to Brackenfold on the left, take a public footpath on the left between beech hedges. This soon reaches a surfaced drive. Turn right for 25 yards then turn left up a public footpath signed to Applethwaite Hill. This goes steeply up a surfaced drive to a gate. The path continues to the right of the gate to a stile over a wall and then on up between fences to another stile over a wall.

3. Turn right and follow the path to the drive to a house called Elleray Bank. Turn right for 20 yards and then left to continue on the footpath to a track. Cross the track and continue beside the wall for 50 yards.

4. Turn left on a walled track and follow this uphill, ignoring a track coming in from the right, until it approaches the edge of the wood. As the track approaches the edge of the wood it goes round a sharp right-hand bend. Take a footpath on the left marked by a yellow arrow on a post. This leads to a gate with a stile beside it. There is an excellent view over the gate of the head of Windermere.

5. Do not cross the stile but continue by the wall, just inside the wood. Ignore all the paths on the right. The southern end of Windermere gradually comes into view and there are some seats admirably placed to admire the view. Go through the kissing gate in the wall by the memorial stone to Arthur Henry Heywood, in whose memory Orrest Head was dedicated to public use, and follow the path to the summit.

The view from Orrest Head is panoramic and different in every direction. It is most dramatic to the north and west and there is a plaque to help you identify all the peaks.

The approach to Orrest Head

The usual path up Orrest Head starts just by the railway station. When most visitors arrived by train the ascent of Orrest Head was a deservedly popular walk. Since most visitors now arrive by car it has perhaps lost some of its popularity but the views are still magnificent.

The town seen below is, of course, Windermere. This walk goes all round it without actually visiting it. Windermere is very much the product of the railway era. The train stopped at the hamlet of Birthwaite but I suppose that didn't sound very attractive to early tourists so the emerging town was called Windermere to emphasize its connection with the lake even though it is some distance away. It was originally planned that the railway should continue on to Ambleside and Grasmere then up over Dunmail Raise to Keswick. This expansion was prevented by the vehement protests of Wordsworth, among others. If the plans had been carried through then Windermere almost certainly would not have developed as much as it has.

6. From the summit, take the path on the side away from the lake heading towards a white building seen below. Go over a stile and follow the sometimes faint path round the hill, still heading towards the white building. At the bottom of the hill, just in front of a small rocky knoll, the path bears right in the direction of the next farm. Cross a stream and in a few yards turn right at a wall corner. (If you arrive at a metal gate with a stile beside it onto a road, you have gone 50 yards too far.)

7. Walk with the wall on the left. The path is not apparent on the ground but goes to a stile over the wall 10 yards right from the corner of the field. In the next field it bears diagonally left to a stile in the far corner. Continue along the left-hand side of the third field to a gate onto a track.

8. Turn right to a farm. After passing by farm buildings, leave the track left to go up to a gate onto a lane.

9. Turn right and follow the lane to the main road. Take a public footpath directly opposite, following the line shown by the sign, slightly right. At a track turn left. When the track forks, bear right.

10. At a gate across the track, do not go through the gate but go over a ladder stile on the left. Walk with the wall on the right and when the wall ends turn right to a stile and a crossing over the railway. Follow the path down and go over a stile on the left onto a lane.

11. Turn right and after 100 yards take a surfaced track on the left signed as a public footpath to School Knott. Carry on along this track until a house on the left called Old Droome is reached.

12. Just after this take a public footpath signed to Lickbarrow on the right. The path crosses a stream and then goes across a field. It is not very clear on the ground but goes straight ahead towards a gate. Do not go through this gate but follow the wall round to the left and continue by the wall to a stile onto a lane.

13. Turn right for 10 yards and then left on a public footpath. Turn left at a cross path signed to Bowness and continue on this path until it joins a track at Helm Farm.

14. Turn left and after 30 yards, when the track bends right, continue through a small wooden gate bearing diagonally right on a path marked by yellow arrows. This comes to a drive. Turn left and in 50 yards come to another drive. Go across this to a kissing gate by a field gate and follow this path into Bowness ignoring all side paths and crossing another drive and a track. This is the Dales Way and is signed as such. It passes a sign saying 81 miles to Ilkley by a slab seat placed to admire the view over Bowness. Join the road and continue down into Bowness, bearing left at the church down to the lake shore.

Bowness is an ancient town dating back to a tenth century Viking settlement. There has been a church on the site of St Martin's for at least 1000 years. The old church was destroyed by fire and the present one and the rectory date from the fifteenth century. Some of the glass from the old church was incorporated into the present east window and the font shows signs of the fire. In the churchyard is the moving grave of forty-seven people drowned when the ferry to Sawrey capsized in 1635. At that time the ferry was a large rowing boat known as the *Great Boat*. During the evening of 19 October 1635 a large party was returning from a wedding at Hawkshead. Over fifty people and eight horses were crammed into the Great Boat and it is not surprising that it capsized and sank.

Bowness was becoming a popular tourist destination even before the arrival of the railway at Birthwaite, just up the road. Birthwaite developed into Windermere and the two towns, the ancient and the new, joined together in an unplanned sprawl.

15. Return past the church and go left along Rayrigg Road for three-quarters of a mile. (For the Hedgerow Tearoom, continue on uphill and the tearoom is about 200 yards up on the right-hand side.)

Windermere Steam Boat Museum was opened in 1979 and houses an interesting collection of historic boats including *Dolly*, the oldest mechanically-powered boat in the world, built in 1850 and raised in 1962 after sixty years under water. *L'Esperance*, the boat used by H.W. Schneider to commute to work at Barrow (see Walk 1, page 15) is also on display here together with many other interesting exhibits, all with some connection with the Lakes.

The museum is open between Easter and the end of October from 10.00am to 5.00pm. Tel. 015394 45565.

16. Take a permissive path on the left to the lake shore. Turn right along the lake shore. When the path forks bear left and continue along the lake shore to a cottage.

17. Turn right away from the lake shore and follow the path up by the stream passing a pretty series of cascades to the road.

From this point, a short detour will take you to the second classic viewpoint over Windermere, Queen Adelaide's Hill. Turn right along the road for 45 yards to a gate on the right and then follow the path to the top of the hill. Retrace your steps.

The hill was named in honour of the visit of the dowager Queen Adelaide in 1840. Queen Adelaide was the consort of William IV who had died three years before, bringing Victoria to the throne. From the summit is a superb view of much of the lake with the Langdales, Wetherlam and the Fairfield range beyond.

18. Turn left along the road back to the starting point.

5. *Ravenglass*

Route:	This is an unusual walk as it visits the Lake District's sea side! The National Park goes as far as the coast in this area and the ancient town of Ravenglass, which was a Roman port, is inside the National Park. The walk also visits Muncaster Castle and has extensive views to the western fells.
Teashop:	The Buttery in the old stables of Muncaster Castle is open from 11.00am to 5.00pm from Easter to the end of October. It has some tables outside and serves a wide range of cakes.
Tel:	01229 717432
Distance:	3½ miles
How to get there:	From the A595 Cumbria coast road, take the side road to Ravenglass. Go under two railway bridges and follow the main road round into the car park.
Start:	Ravenglass car park. SD 085965

1. Take the path at the far left-hand corner of the car park over the railway line and follow the path to a surfaced drive.

2. Turn right, signed to Newtown Knott and Muncaster, and walk along this for half a mile passing Walls Castle on the left.

Walls Castle is the remains of the bath house of the Roman fort of Glannaventa. It is the only part of the fort still visible and the walls still stand 12½ feet high, the tallest Roman remains in the North of England. It probably owes its remarkable state of preservation to the fact that The

Pennington family used it as a home until they became rich enough to build Muncaster Castle in the fourteenth century.

Glannaventa was the Western end of the Roman road from Ambleside over Hard Knott. It served as the port for the area and for the Isle of Man and may have been developed as a supply base for an intended invasion of Ireland, which never happened. The Romans probably built on an existing port because Glanna means 'town on the bank' in ancient British and 'venta' comes from the Latin for 'place of commerce'.

Walls Castle

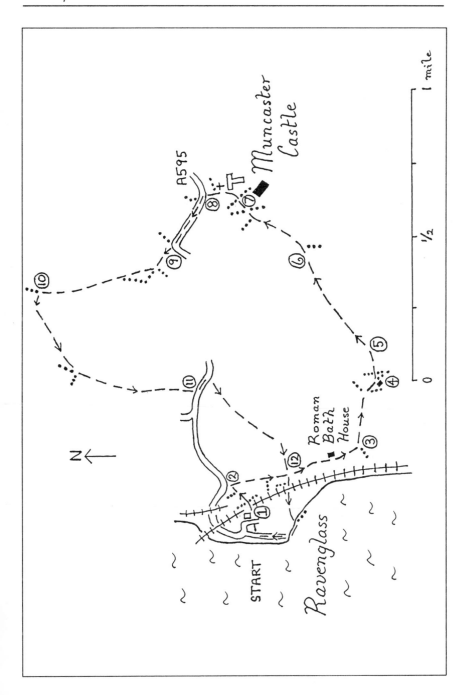

Walls Castle was identified as the bath house in 1928 and an
explanatory plaque on the site shows the extent of the rest of
the fort which accommodated as many as 1000 men. The civil
settlement stretched north on much the same site as the
present town of Ravenglass.

3. 100 yards after the bath house, turn left on a track signed to
   Newtown Cottage and follow this, ignoring all side turns.

4. At Newtown Cottage take a permissive path through a gate with
   a sign on the left. After 20 yards cross another path to continue
   uphill through a conifer plantation to a stile.

5. Over the stile the path is not apparent on the ground. It goes half
   left to a broken stile and then continues in the same direction
   between two low hills with a view of the Lake District fells beyond.
   As the ground begins to fall slightly, veer right towards a wall
   enclosing trees. As you get closer to this look for a post sticking
   up as this marks the position of a gate in the wall.

6. Go through the gate and continue on the path, now going downhill.
   You are now in the Muncaster Castle Gardens and should not
   deviate from the public footpath unless you buy a ticket. However,
   the gardens are well worth exploring, especially in late spring
   when the rhododendrons and azaleas are in bloom. At the bottom
   of the hill cross a track and walk by the duck pond. At the surfaced
   drive you may deviate right off the public footpath for a few yards
   to the tea shop and you are welcome to do this.

   Muncaster Castle is the ancestral home of the Pennington
   family. They have owned it since they moved from their Roman
   bath house in the fourteenth century and developed a defensive
   pele tower into a castle in 1325. The castle was incorporated
   into the present structure for the fourth Lord Muncaster
   between 1862 and 1866 by Anthony Salvin, a Victorian
   architect who specialised in modernising castles. The building
   contains many interesting portraits including one of Thomas

Skelton, the last and most famous Fool of Muncaster. His pranks and friendship with Shakespeare are the origin of the expression 'tom fool'.

Also on display is a replica of the Luck of Muncaster, an enamelled and gilded glass bowl. There are several other glass bowls found in Lakeland also known as 'lucks' which are supposed to bring their owners good fortune. Often they are reputed to be gifts of the fairies but the origin of the Muncaster Luck is more earthly and better documented. Henry VI was lost on Muncaster Fell after the battle of Hexham in 1464 during the Wars of the Roses. He was found by a shepherd and brought to Muncaster Castle where the Penningtons sheltered him for nine days. In gratitude he gave the family a drinking bowl with the promise that as long it remained intact, the Penningtons would live and thrive at Muncaster – and so they have!

The position of Muncaster Castle is unsurpassed. The gardens are well worth exploring, if you have time, especially in late spring. The view from the terrace into the mountains is widely reckoned to be one of the finest in Britain.

The gardens are open all through the year between 11.00am and 5.00pm. The castle is open Tuesday to Sunday and Bank Holiday Mondays from 1.00pm to 4.00pm.

7. From the tea shop, turn right up the surfaced drive to the road, passing the garden centre and Muncaster church.

Muncaster church was started in the 12th century though there is an older preaching cross in the church yard. More information is available, as usual, within.

8. At the road turn left for 350 yards.

9. When the road bends sharp left, continue in the same direction on a track signed 'Public Footpath — Muncaster Mill and Branken Wall'. In a dip, just before the farm, take a permitted bridleway on the right signed to Muncaster Mill.

10. When the track forks, bear left as directed by a yellow arrow on a post. At a crossing track turn left and follow this through three gates to a road.

11. Turn left for 120 yards and then take a public footpath on the right. Follow the path through the wood and then across a field. The path is not very apparent in the field but goes ahead and slightly left to a gate. Through the gate turn right and walk along the right-hand side of the field to a drive.

12. This is the same drive you walked along near the start of the walk. The return route goes straight across this drive and along a public footpath opposite, under the railway and on to the shore. Continue in the same direction along the shore to the bottom of the main street and then turn left along the main street. Take a public footpath on the right just in front of the Pennington Arms signed 'Railway Station'. This leads back to the car park where the walk started.

Ravenglass is an ancient port, probably in existence before the Romans came. Its position at the confluence of three rivers — the Irt, the Mite and the Esk — meant it was a wonderful natural harbour for shallow draft boats. As long as the pack horse was the main means of transporting goods into and out of the central Lakes, Ravenglass had a secure position as an important port. The development of other means of transport, the canals and then the railway, and the coming of ships with a deeper draft spelt the end of Ravenglass and the last iron ore was shipped from its rapidly silting harbour in the 1880s. The encroaching sands which have doomed Ravenglass as a modern port are of great importance for wildlife and there are nature reserves to both the north and south of the town.

The ancient street, now a conservation area with a pleasing wide variety of buildings, runs down onto the sands in a curious and unusual way. The reason for this is that this was once one of the main routes into the town from the south, as the sands were no problem for pack horses. The line of the road today is dictated by the needs of modern transport. It is also narrow at the end to prevent the escape of animals on market day.

Ravenglass was granted its market charter in 1208 when this was an important three-day event with traders coming from far and near. As the importance of Ravenglass declined, so did the fair. By the end of the eighteenth century it was down to one day and by the end of the nineteenth century, it had finished altogether.

Ravenglass is also the home of the Ravenglass and Eskdale Railway or 'Ratty' (see walk 13, page 82) and there is a museum with information about the line near the station.

Note: at very high tides the path along the shore will be covered. On these rare occasions retrace your steps to the starting point by turning right along the drive.

6. Tarn Hows and Coniston

Route:	This walk is through typical Lakeland scenery and visits one of the best-loved beauty spots. It is not long but plenty of time should be allowed as there are two sharp climbs.
Teashop:	There are several teashops to choose from in Coniston. Coniston Dairy has an excellent range of cakes and a full afternoon tea with sandwiches, scones and cakes on the menu. It is open until 5.30pm throughout the year and there are some tables outside.
Tel:	015394 41319
Distance:	6 miles. The walk can be extended by 1½ miles by taking the path around Tarn Hows.
How to get there:	From the A593 Ambleside to Coniston road, take a minor road signed 'Hodge Close only'.
Start:	150 yards from the junction there is space for several cars to park. SD 314998

1. Walk along the lane and over the bridge and immediately turn right through a gate. After about half a mile the path goes behind a farm and then comes to a gate. Go through the gate, ignoring a rising track to the left, and down to the road.

2. Turn left along the road for 200 yards as far as a bridge, ignoring a path on the right just before the bridge. Cross the beck by the footbridge and keep the beck on the right as you walk uphill. Just before the second waterfall, fork right to stay by the beck to Tarn Hows.

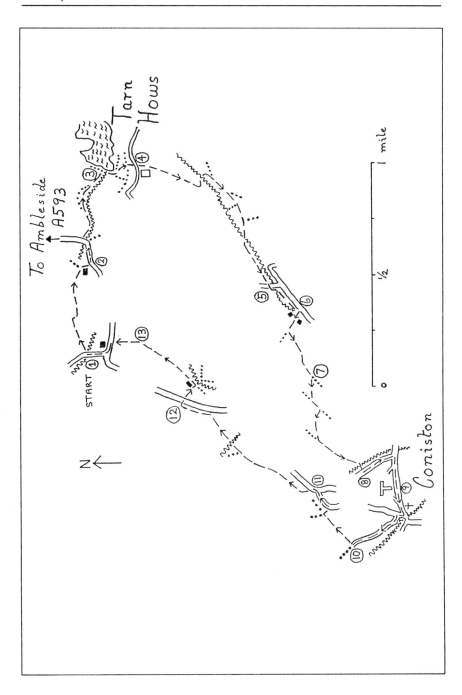

Tarn Hows

Tarn Hows is the great tourist honey pot of this part of the Lake District, attracting about a million visitors annually. It is extremely attractive with the jewel-like tarn framed in a backdrop of trees and hills and all very accessible from the car! A National Trust survey carried out to help formulate a management plan found that most visitors do not walk far from their cars, however.

People are often surprised to learn that Tarn Hows is not a natural feature. Originally there were two tarns called, with great creativity, High Tarn and Low Tarn. Tarn Hows was the name of a nearby farm. The Marshall family who owned Monk Coniston Hall dammed the area to make a single larger body of water and planted the surrounds with trees so that it conformed with the then fashionable ideas of Arcadian beauty which so many obviously still find attractive today. Paths were laid round the tarn and linking the new garden with the existing gardens of Monk Coniston Hall.

In 1930 the Monk Coniston Estate was put up for sale by the Marshall family. Beatrix Potter bought the whole estate to save it from afforestation or other development. She sold half to the National Trust at cost and kept the other half for herself but bequeathing it to the Trust. An appeal was launched to raise money to buy the Trust's half which quickly reached the necessary sum. There were lots of small donations and some large ones including one in particular from the Scott family as a memorial to Lord and Lady Scott.

The surrounding area is full of wildlife interest and is a national Site of Special Scientific Interest. The National Trust has to balance the demands of the hoards of visitors as well as conservation of the wildlife. An important means towards this is the provision and maintenance of good paths which people tend to stay on, rather than wandering into more biologically sensitive areas.

3. Turn right at Tarn Hows and follow the middle of three paths up to the road. (Turn left to walk around Tarn Hows.)

4. Cross the road and take the path to the left of the National Trust car park. This goes gently downhill, crossing two small streams, and winds its way down to the valley bottom where it crosses the main stream. Continue with the stream on the right and bear right at a fork. Recross the stream and continue with the stream on the left to a minor road.

5. Cross the road and go through a gate on the other side signed 'Footpath to Coniston'. Recross the stream and go ahead with the stream on the right to emerge on a road.

6. Turn right and after 25 yards turn right again between buildings. 60 yards after the last building turn left over a stile by a wooden gate and follow the path uphill to a gate. Continue uphill through a wood.

To the left from this path are good views of Coniston Water.
The lake is five miles long and just over 180 feet deep at the
deepest part. It is remarkably straight and for this reason was
used by the Campbells for the water speed records. The father,
Malcolm Campbell set a record of 141.76mph in his Bluebird in
1939. His son, Donald, increased the record to 276.33mph and
was attempting to surpass this when he was tragically killed on
the morning of 4 January 1967 as his boat either hit a
submerged log or became airborne and somersaulted. No one
really knows what happened and his body was never recovered.

7. When the path forks, bear right on a permissive path. Continue
   climbing to join a path from the right. Turn left for about 100 yards
   and then turn right to follow a clear path which soon goes downhill
   and over a stile to join another path. Turn left and follow the path
   downhill to a bridge and the road.

8. Turn left and then right into Coniston at the T-junction. Coniston
   Dairy is on the right.

Coniston village is the product of the mining industry. The
slopes of Coniston Old man behind are riddled with old workings.
The copper ores were probably first mined by the Romans. In the
second half of the sixteenth century, German miners came
from Keswick and mining increased in intensity after 1758 when
the Macclesfield Copper Company acquired the lease of the
mines. Copper is not easy to smelt and it was always exported
from Coniston for smelting. At first, the ore was carried by
pack horse to Keswick where copper was smelted at Brigham on
the River Greta. Later it was exported by water, down the lake
and then by horse and cart to the ports of Ulverston or
Greenodd to be smelted in Wales. Understandably, there was
considerable pressure for a railway link which arrived in 1859.

The most prosperous period for copper mining in Coniston was
in the 1830s and 1850s when Cornish technology, capital and

expertise were introduced. At its height the industry employed some nine hundred men, women and children who produced about two hundred and fifty tons a week. It went into a decline, however, and by the 1880s had all but finished. Today Coniston is a tourist centre attracting large numbers of visitors.

The scenery round Coniston is a good illustration of the effects of geology on landscape. To the north and west are craggy Borrowdale Volcanic rocks which contained the copper ores while to the south and east are the more easily eroded Silurian Slates which produce a gentler landscape (see page 2).

9. From the tea shop, continue along the road. Turn right just before the bridge and take the first road on the left after 40 yards by the Black Bull.

10. A few yards after the road deteriorates into a track, take an unsigned path on the right over a stile. Continue ahead with a dry stone wall on the right. After about 400 yards turn right through a gate in the wall and go down between buildings to a minor road. Turn left.

11. At the main road, turn left for 50 yards and then go through a gap in the wall on the left onto a permissive path through woodland. After about half a mile the path crosses White Gill by a footbridge. White Gill can be spectacular after rain as it tumbles down the fell side. Carry on along this footpath over two stiles and alongside the road as far as Low Yewdale.

12. Opposite the track to Low Yewdale, go down some steps onto the road and take the public bridleway directly opposite to the farm. Turn left immediately after the barn, before the bridge, and go in front of the cottages. Follow the path across the fields. The path is not obvious on the ground but goes from gate to gate across three fields.

13. In the fourth field turn left along the left-hand side of the field to the farm and the road. At the road turn left and in 100 yards turn right, back to the starting point.

7. *Hawkshead*

Route: This is a walk of contrasts. The first part, before tea, is through woodland on tracks and the return is across fields which can be very muddy after prolonged rain. The wise walker will therefore be prepared for mud or save this walk for drier weather. Throughout there are wonderful views.

Teashop: Hawkshead has several teashops. The Minstrel's Gallery is a classic teashop in a fifteenth century building that was once a pub — the Crown and Mitre. It offers an excellent selection of cakes and serves a full afternoon tea of sandwiches, scones, malt loaf and cakes. It is open from 10.30am until 5.30pm every day except Friday from mid-February to mid-December.

Tel: 015394 36423

Distance: 6 miles

How to get there: From Ambleside take the A593 Coniston road. At Clappersgate turn left on the B5286 to Hawkshead. After 1½ miles take a minor road on the left signed 'Wray 1¼ miles and Wray Castle and campsite'. Drive down this road for about a mile to the entrance to Wray Castle. There are parking spaces at the side of the road just beyond.

Start: Gates of Wray Castle. NY 372007

1. With your back to the entrance to Wray Castle turn left and walk along the lane for about half a mile through the hamlet of High Wray.

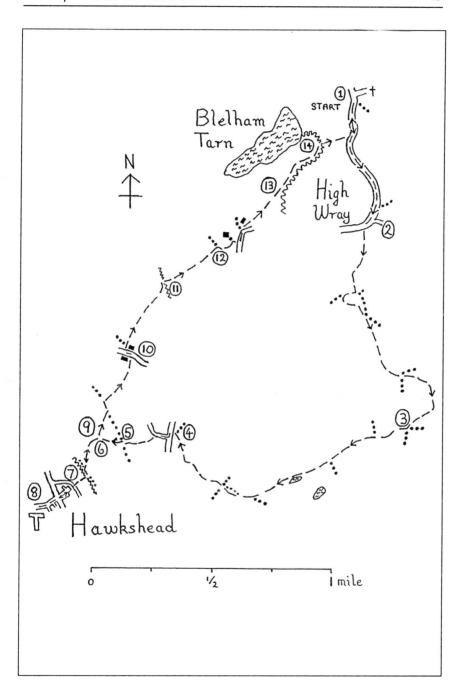

Wray Castle sometimes deceives people with its medieval appearance but it is actually a Victorian extravaganza. It was built in the 1840s for a Liverpool doctor, Dr. James Dawson. It was rented by Bearix Potter's family as a holiday home and it was then that the family became acquainted with Canon Rawnsley who was the vicar of Wray at that time. Canon Rawnsley was one of the founders of the National Trust and was a considerable influence on Beatrix Potter. He suggested that she send 'The Tale of Peter Rabbit' to Frederick Warne and Co. who eventually published all her books.

Wray Castle is now in the care of the National Trust. The castle itself is occupied by a Merchant Navy training school and is not open to the public.

2. Pass a road on the left and after 100 yards turn left on a track signed 'National Trust Basecamp'. This climbs gently upwards and gives wonderful views of Windermere behind as you turn to admire the view. Continue on up the track past the entrance to the Basecamp and over a stile by a gate. Bear right when the track forks just after a rough track joins on the right.

3. At a cross-paths marked by signposts, turn right on a public bridleway signed to Hawkshead. At the next junction in about 250 yards, go through the gate and stay on the track. Follow the track as it goes gently downhill for about a mile altogether. After about three-quarters of a mile, the track forks: bear left by the wall and shortly continue across a crossing path. Hawkshead can now be seen ahead.

4. At the road turn left for 50 yards and then turn right. In another 75 yards turn left on a signed public footpath which soon goes through a gate into a field. The path bears right to a stile in a stone wall just where it joins a wire fence and then continues in the same direction to another stile almost in the far right corner of the field. It then goes steeply down to a small gate onto a track.

5. Go through a small gate almost directly opposite and follow the path ahead across the field to another gate. ** Note this point well – it is referred to in instruction 8.

6. Go through the gate and bear slightly left to yet another gate and across a further field to a footbridge over the river. Follow the track on the other side to the road.

7. Cross the road and go through a small gate opposite between buildings into Hawkshead. The Minstrels Gallery Tea Room is ahead and to the left and is well-signed.

The Minstrels' Gallery Tea Rooms

It is well worth spending some time exploring Hawkshead, now one of the Lake District's most picturesque villages and formerly a town of considerable importance. It contains thirty-eight buildings of special architectural or historic interest and only residents' cars are allowed in the village centre.

Hawkshead started as a Norse settlement called *Hawkr's saeter,* a saeter being a summer farm. Furness Abbey owned all the land from Windermere to Coniston and encouraged the wool trade. This was the source of Hawkshead's wealth. The town received its market charter in 1608 and for the next two hundred years was the main centre for the trade in wool. This was very profitable especially for the farmers or statesmen who acquired their own land after the dissolution of Furness Abbey in 1537. This accounts for the many fine seventeenth century buildings in Hawkshead.

One of the most famous is the Grammar school founded in 1585 by the Archbishop of York, Edwin Sandys. The Sandys family is still a local landowner. The present building, dating from 1675, is open to the public. William Wordsworth attended the school from 1779 to 1787 and wrote one of his earliest poems for its bicentenary. More prosaically, he also carved his initials on his desk. This piece of vandalism is now preserved for posterity under glass. The house where he lodged with Anne Tyson can also be seen though there is some dispute about how long Wordsworth actually lived there because the Tyson's also had property at Colthouse near Hawkshead.

In Wordworth's day the ancient church of St Michael and All Angels was painted with whitewash, but this was removed when it was restored in 1875. Fortunately, the superb series of wall paintings dating from 1680 was preserved. The church has many interesting features. Near the North door is an interesting record of burial: to promote the wool trade, Parliament passed an Act in 1666 that corpses had to be wrapped in a wool shroud rather than linen or silk.

Main Street has two properties owned by the National Trust. The Information Centre is in 'Bump or Bend' which gets its name from the difficulty that buses and lorries once had getting past the overhanging first storey. Next door were the offices of William Heelis, Beatrix Potter's solicitor husband. They have now been converted into a Beatrix Potter gallery. The Red Lion, which you need to find to continue the walk, is also on Main Street. It has a stylish Victorian facade built in 1850 which reflects the fact that by that date tourism had replaced wool as the main money spinner for this prosperous little town.

8. Retrace your steps to the point marked ** in instruction 5, above, by going through the arch to the right of the Red Lion Inn.

9. Turn left on the path signed to Loanthwaite. Cross a stile and bear right to a small gate onto a track. Turn left for 60 yards then go through a small gate on the right. Go up the right-hand side of the field to a stile by a gate and then up the right-hand side of the next field. Near the end of the field go through a gate on the right and continue in the same direction, now with the hedge on the left, to a gate onto a lane by a farm.

10. Turn left for 100 yards and go through a gate on the right at the end of the farm buildings on a public footpath signed to Outgate and High Wray. Keep on the track signed 'Footpath to Tock How and High Wray' to a stile by a gate. Continue ahead, initially with a line of trees on the left, to a stile. There is a dyke across the direct line but this can be crossed near the fence.

11. Continue on the footpath which is just discernible on the ground and helpfully marked by arrows on posts.

12. Turn right through a gate and follow the track to the entrance to the farm. Turn right to the public road and then left along it. After 100 yards leave the road and go in front of some buildings. Follow the clear track ahead to a stile.

13. Over the stile the way is less obvious but follows the field boundary round to the right, over another stile and continues along the right-hand side of the field through a copse to a bridge over a stream.

14. Again continue along the right-hand side of the field to the road and turn left for a few yards back to the starting point.

8. Jenkin Crag and Waterhead

Route:	This is a short but quite energetic walk which climbs up to the spectacular viewpoint of Jenkin Crag and then passes by Stagshaw Gardens which are in the care of the National Trust. It returns along the lakeside passing through Waterhead and by the site of a Roman fort.
Teashop:	There are several tea shops in Waterhead and many of the hotels there also serve afternoon tea so there is something for all tastes and budgets. The Waterhead Coffee Shop is in a fine position overlooking the lake by the jetties. It is open from March to November from 10.00am to 5.30pm and has tables outside to enjoy the view across the lake. It also sells duck food!
Tel:	015394 32038
Distance:	3 miles
How to get there:	Take the A5075 between Ambleside and Waterhead. Watch for a public car park about half-way between them not far from the garden centre but on the opposite side of the road.
Start:	Low Fold car park. NY 377038

1. Leave the car park at the rear and turn right. Take the first left signed 'Jenkins Crag, Skelghyll and Troutbeck'. Follow the track up and when it forks take the right branch signed to Jenkyns Crag. The track contours along the hill side with superb views on the left over the head of Windermere and up Langdale Valley. At the next fork again take the right option to continue along the hill side.

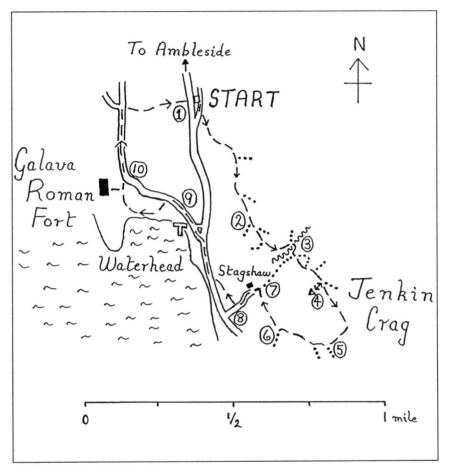

2. On entering Skelghyll Woods, ignore a path on the right to con-
    tinue uphill on the main path. Pass the private entrance to Skel-
    ghyll Wood and then fork left on a path signed to Jenkyns Crag
    and Troutbeck.

3. Join a crossing path and turn right to cross the beck. Ignore all
    paths on the right and left and continue up to Jenkyns Crag. Turn
    right through a gap in the wall at the Jenkyn's Crag sign to the
    view point.

Jenkin Crag has magnificent views over the head of Windermere and the fells beyond. The exact spelling of the name seems to vary. On the Ordnance Survey map it is called Jenkin Crag. The sign on the track near the start directs us to 'Jenkins Crag' and further up the spelling has changed to 'Jenkyns Crag'.

4. From the view point return towards the main path. Just before the gap in the wall, take a smaller path on the right downhill. As it approaches a stone wall this makes a sharp right turn to continue steeply downhill through an area of newly planted trees.

5. Turn right on a crossing path and then right again at a second crossing path.

6. When the path turns very sharply left, continue in the same direction on a smaller path. Follow this to join a track.

7. Turn left to pass Stagshaw Gardens on the right after 50 yards.

Stagshaw Gardens were created by the late C.H.D. Acland, a keen gardener, who was regional agent for the National Trust for nearly thirty years. An area of scrubby woodland was transformed into a series of glades with rhododendrons, azaleas and a wide variety of other shrubs thriving under the thinned oaks. It is essentially a spring garden and is open every day from April until the end of June from 10.00am to 6.30pm. In the summer, from July to October, it is open by appointment only. (Applications in writing to the National Trust Regional Office in Grasmere.)

8. Just after a stone barn on the left turn right on a path between walls and follow this to the road. Turn right. There is a footway on the opposite side of this busy road. At the traffic lights bear left and the various teashops and hotels are all round here.

Waterhead is a group of houses and hotels built on Windermere near Ambleside to cater for the Victorian tourists who were the first to flock here and it still fulfils that function today. The Windermere steamers call here and go to Bowness and Lakeside (see Walk 1 on page 15 and Walk 4 on page 33). There are also launches for shorter cruises on the lake.

9. Continue by the lake side passing the Wateredge Hotel. Just after the hotel turn left into the park and continue in the same direction, parallel with the road. At the far end of the park go through a metal kissing gate in the wall to Borran's Field containing the remains of the Roman fort.

The Romans invaded Britain in 55 and 54 B.C. but it was not until 78 to 79 A.D. that they really took on the North. The excavator of this site, R.G. Collingwood, thought thar the fort had been started in about 79 A.D. but it is now thought to have been built in the late 90s in the reign of Emperor Trajan.

The first fort was a timber and turf structure. The site is excellent from a strategic point of view but was liable to flooding so it was then rebuilt in stone on a raised platform which can still be seen. It was in the shape of a playing card and measured 395 feet by 270 feet. It was surrounded by a stone wall 12 to 15 feet high with rounded corners and turrets at each corner. There was a gate in each wall.

The one in the East wall was the main gate or Porta Praetoria and the remains of this are in the first small fenced area you come to. Inside the gate, the Via Praetoria went straight on for 50 yards to the HQ buildings in the centre of the fort and these are the other remains to be seen in the fenced areas ahead. From left to right, they are the Commander's house, the HQ building and the granaries. The HQ building was flanked by L-shaped armories with a basilica or main hall with three rooms behind: a chapel where the standards and treasury were kept and offices. The granaries on the right are easily recognised because they were built on a lattice of low walls. The other buildings inside the fort were the barracks. No trace of these remains visible on the ground as they were built of wood.

Galava Fort

Galava fort was manned by five hundred auxiliaries. It is not really accurate to imagine Romans shivering under Lakeland drizzle trying to suppress rebellious locals. To begin with they did come from other parts of the Western Roman Empire such as Gaul and North Africa. Later the auxiliaries were recruited locally, signing on for twenty-five years. The fort mostly existed peacefully with the civilian population and the main problem was marauding Picts and Scots.

Outside the fort were the parade ground and *vicus* or village, where the soldiers' families lived and the bath house was to be found. The site of this bath house has not been found.

The fort was abandoned around 400 A.D. as the Roman Empire collapsed. The name of the site, Borran's Field, is from the

Norse name meaning heap of stones, which suggests the state it was in at that time.

It was bought by the National Trust in 1912 to protect it from house building. It was excavated by R.G. Collingworth between 1914 and 1920. There has been no excavation inside the fort since Collingworth's day.

10. After exploring the fort return to the road and turn left. Opposite the A593 Coniston road, turn right on a public footpath which emerges opposite the starting point.

9. Little Langdale

Route:	Though by no means the longest walk in this book, this must be a serious contender for Most Strenuous Walk. It climbs Lingmoor Fell from Blea Tarn which will give plenty of opportunity to stand and stare at the magnificent views of the Langdales. It then descends to Little Langdale for tea before climbing back to Blea Tarn. On no account should this walk be attempted in poor visibility as this could make route-finding on the summit of Lingmoor Fell very difficult.
Teashop:	The popular pub, the Three Shires Inn, serves teas with excellent scones every day including Sunday afternoon when the bar is shut.
Tel:	019667 215
Distance:	6 miles
How to get there:	Take the B5343 Great Langdale road. At the head of the valley take the minor road left. Just after Blea Tarn there is a car park on the left.
Start:	Blea Tarn car park. NY 296043

1. Turn right along the road for about a quarter of a mile.

2. Watch for a wall on the left coming up from the tarn to join the wall along the left side of the road. After a further 20 yards, take an unsigned path on the right up the fell side.

The ascent of Lingmoor gives the best views of Blea Tarn and it was this view that inspired Wordsworth to write in *The Excursion*:

Behold! Beneath our feet a little lowly vale
A lowly vale, and yet lifted high
Among the mountains -
A liquid pool that glittered in the sun . . .

It is very difficult to appreciate that the wild country we see is
as much a man-made landscape as any city. One of the places
where research has been done into this is Blea Tarn. Pollen
grains are very slow to rot down so by looking at the pollen
grains trapped in sediment at the botton of the tarn we can
tell quite a lot about the vegetation around the tarn at
different times in the past. Until about 3000BC the area was
thickly forested. Neolithic people started the process of cutting
down the trees. The counts of elm pollen fall dramatically and it
is thought they used elm leaves and young shoots as bedding
and fodder for animals. In the silt at the bottom of the tarn is
a layer showing that the removal of the trees led to increased
erosion from the denuded hillsides. Down the centuries this
process continued until the hills were left bare of trees and it is
only in this century that the process of deforrestation has
been slightly reversed.

3. Turn right at a cross path at the edge of a steep tree-lined valley
    to continue uphill, essentially along the right-hand side of this
    valley. The path goes through a gap in the wall and continues up
    steeply. Just as the path levels a little, watch for a path on the right.
    Do not take the first, faint path but take the second more distinct
    one after a further 10 yards. The path straight ahead ends at the
    edge of the steep valley in a few yards so, if you get there, you
    know you have missed the path on the right and must go back and
    look for it.

4. Almost at the head of the valley, the path dips down into the valley
    to a wooden crossing point over a stone wall. Cross this and turn
    left to follow a path uphill by a wall and fence. This leads to a
    crossing fence and the summit cairn.

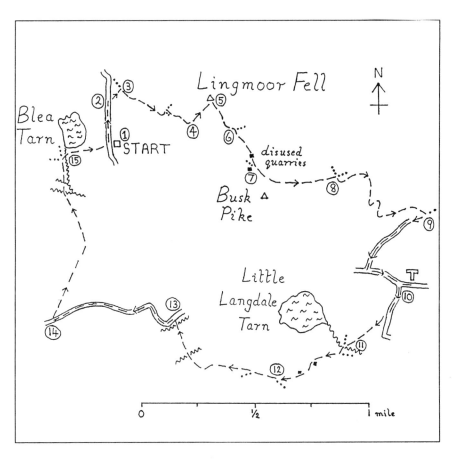

The summit is one of several rocky outcrops, each of which has its own name: this is Brown How. It is a rocky outcrop superimposed with a large cairn. Lingmoor fell gives unparalleled views of the great mountains all around since it is the dividing range between Great and Little Langdale. 'Ling' is an old word for heather and it is from this plant which grows freely round the summit, especially on the northern side, that the fell gets its name. It has been much quarried, as have some of the surrounding hills, for its fine green slate and evidence of this past and present industry will be seen all around.

5. Do not cross the crossing fence except to admire the view into Great Langdale but turn right to follow a path by the fence. Watch for a derelict quarry building down and to the right below a rocky outcrop with a prominent cairn on the top (Busk Pike) as the route eventually makes for this.

6. Just after a short steep descent the fence becomes a wall. Almost immediately bear right on a faint path marked intermittently by cairns. The path passes by another derelict quarry building which cannot be seen from far away. Continue on towards Busk Pike to the derelict quarry building seen from above.

7. Here an excellent, well-engineered path starts, presumably built to get to these now disused buildings. Turn left on this and follow it downhill past some more derelict quarry buildings.

   The views south as you come down this path are magnificent. The large sheet of water in the distance is Windermere. The irregular, smaller body of water rather nearer is Elterwater which is difficult to see in its entirety from many places. The small tarn on the right is Little Langdale Tarn and Coniston can be glimpsed ahead, slightly right.

8. Turn right on a crossing path marked by a cairn and follow this path as it zigzags downhill, eventually joining a track.

9. Turn right. The track soon becomes a farm lane leading to a road. Turn left and follow the road down to the Three Shires Inn and tea.

   The Three Shires Inn gets its name from the three shires stone on Wrynose pass where the old counties of Lancashire, Westmorland and Cumberland met. The coat of arms of the inn has the emblems of these counties.

10. From the inn return up the road for 60 yards and then turn left down a side road signed to Tilberthwaite. After 250 yards, take a path on the right up a few steps. Follow the path round to the left

to a kissing gate and then ahead downhill to a bridge over the stream.

Slater Bridge

This bridge is called Slater Bridge. It is thought to be very old and is a much photographed example of a packhorse bridge. Some were built as an arch and others by laying large slabs of stone across the stream. This bridge is a combination of the two. Little Langdale has long been an important route to the west and the sea (see Walk 10, page 69) and pack ponies were watered at Little Langdale Tarn before starting the arduous climb over Wrynose and Hard Knott passes.

11. Cross the stile over the wall at the far end of the bridge and follow the path to a gate onto a track. Turn right. Follow the track past some buildings and through a gate onto the open fell side.

12. A path joins on the left. Continue in the same direction. When the track forks after another 125 yards bear right and follow it to a road.

13. Turn left for about half a mile.

Behind Fell Foot Farm is a low grassy mound which is supposed to be a Thing Mount – a Norse parliament meeting place. At the time of writing it had a washing line on it!

14. As the wall on the left finishes, take a footpath on the right. This is very indistinct to begin with as it crosses a boggy area but it soon becomes clearer and drier as it enters bracken. Follow this path to the tarn passing by a very pretty series of small cascades.

15. On reaching the tarn turn right over the stream by a log bridge and follow the path back to the car park.

10. The Waterfalls

Route:	This walk starts in the village of Elterwater and visits two of the best waterfalls in the Lake District, so it is a walk for after a spell of rain. There are some excellent views.
Teashop:	The Kirkstone Galleries at Skelwith Bridge has an excellent tea shop with a wide range of home-made cakes and tables outside in summer. It is open from 10.00am to 5.30pm in summer but closes earlier in winter.
Tel:	015394 34002
Distance:	5 miles
How to get there:	From Ambleside take the A593 Coniston road. At Skelwith Bridge, bear right on the B5343 Langdales road. Just after a cattle grid, turn left into Elterwater village. The car park is just before the river on the left.
Start:	The National Trust car park in Elterwater village. NY 327047

Elterwater village is an attractive cluster of houses round the Britannia Inn. It is separated from the main road, the B5343 by a large open common which is owned by the National Trust. The village was once a centre for the manufacture of gunpowder. Production started in 1824 and continued until after the first World War. The works were powered by six water wheels and the site is now a holiday complex.

1. Return to the road and turn left over the river. Continue on the road for 300 yards, past the Youth Hostel and the entrance to Eltermere Hall Hotel, and then fork right. When the road bends right, continue

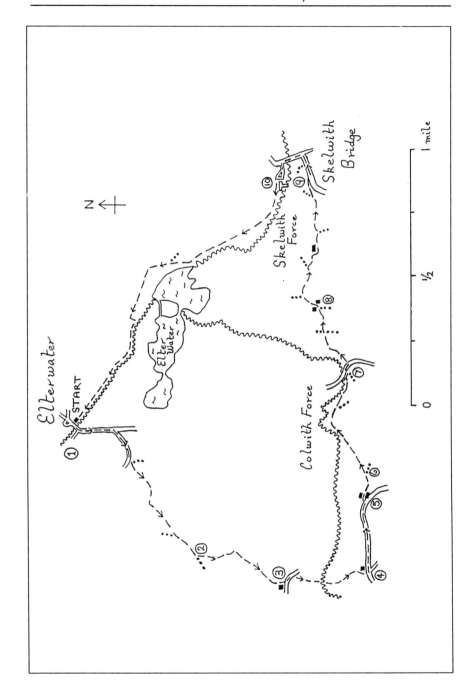

ahead on a track between walls, climbing first steeply and then more gently for about half a mile. Ignore all paths on the right and left. There are some superb views on the left as the path rises.

2. Just over the brow of the hill turn left on a public footpath. This leads to a stone stile and then bends right to a second stile and down the right-hand side of a field to a farm. Go through the farm yard to a lane.

This valley is Little Langdale. In Roman times, it was a major route to the west and the sea as the Tenth Highway went along the valley from Ambleside. The road continues to the right through the hamlet of Little Langdale and by Little Langdale Tarn and then rises up over the wild pass of Wrynose. Wilson Place, whose farm yard you have just walked through, can be traced back to 1645 when it was owned by Isaac Wilson. He was a Wilson of Kendal, still noted for their mint cake!

3. Turn left for 80 yards and then take a signed path on the right through a kissing gate. Follow the path downhill across the field to a bridge and then up the other side of the valley to a farm. The path turns right in front of the farm to a lane.

4. Turn left and immediately fork left and walk along the lane as far as the next farm, just over a quarter of a mile.

5. Take a path on the left through a gate into the farm yard. Go between farm buildings to a gate and follow the path across a field to a kissing gate next to a field gate. Turn left and walk along the left-hand side of the field and into the wood.

6. Just inside the wood, fork left on a permissive path to Colwith Force and then continue on the same path by the river to a road.

Colwith Force is almost hidden among the trees and, when it is in spate, can be heard before it is seen. The water cascades over 90 feet in two main leaps.

7. Turn right for 75 yards and then take a public footpath on the left over a stone stile signed to Skelwith Bridge. Follow the clear path across the field, up a short steep climb and across a second field to emerge on a track. Cross the track and continue on the footpath to a farm.

8. Go through the farm yard and continue on a track. After 75 yards, turn right. The path is very clear and easy to follow. 100 yards after some cottages bear left and follow the path into a wood. At a fork, bear right to a road.

9. Turn left and follow the road over the bridge to Kirkstone Galleries and the tea room.

The evidence of slate quarrying, both past and present, can be seen all around this part of the Lakes. The slate, known as Westmorland Green, has been used as a building material since Roman times. Its structure means that it can be split into thin sheets with a hammer and chisel making it very suitable as a roofing material. Slate was superseded by cheaper alternatives and many of the district's quarries were forced to close. However, the beauty of the stone and modern technology which means that even thinner sheets can be cut has enabled the industry to continue as it can be used for wall cladding and floors as well as the traditional roofing. It is also made into a wide variety of objects, some of which are displayed in the showroom.

10. On leaving the tea room turn left and go between the buildings to pick up a path by the river and Skelwith Force to a gate. The path across the field is not always clear on the ground but go straight across the field and the path soon becomes much more obvious as it approaches the river bank. It reaches the shore of Elterwater and then goes through a gate into a wood. It is then a clear and easy-to-follow path through the wood and alongside the river back to Elterwater.

Skelwith Force is the second waterfall on the River Brathay. A fault in the bed of the river has produced a drop of sixteen feet. This isn't very high but it is very dramatic as the water pours over it in a solid mass. There were once bobbin mills at Skelwith driven by water from the fall – part of the old leat is still visible.

Elterwater is one of the smaller lakes and not easy to see fully. It was once much larger than it is now and is slowly being filled in by material eroded from the fells above and carried down by streams. All the water draining from the Great and Little Langdale Fells drains through Elterwater. The only path along its shore is the one we take. This doesn't give a good view of the lake but the views to the Langdale Pikes beyond are magnificent.

Elterwater gets its name from the Norse word 'eltra' meaning 'swan' so this is Swan Lake! It is visited by whooper swans in winter.

'Swan Lake'

11. Grasmere

Route:	This walk starts by exploring the lower slopes of Silver Howe, the fell that separates Grasmere from Langdale. It climbs up to a viewpoint with unsurpassed views over Grasmere, passing a pretty little waterfall on the way. It returns to Grasmere village with a short walk back to the starting point after tea.
Teashop:	There are, of course, many tea shops in Grasmere which with its literary connections is a mecca for tourists both British and foreign and therefore rarely to be enjoyed peacefully. Baldry's has excellent cakes and other tea time goodies. It has a few tables outside and is open every day in the summer from 9.00am to 6.00pm.
Tel:	015394 35301
Distance:	3 miles
How to get there:	From the A591 Ambleside to Keswick road, take the B5287 through Grasmere village. Take the minor road called Easedale Road and signed to Easedale Tarn.
Start:	Easedale Road car park. NY 334080

1. Cross the road to join a permissive path and turn right to rejoin the road just before the river.

2. At Goody Bridge Farm, turn left on a public footpath. This goes through the garden in front of cottages, through a gate and down the right-hand side of a field to cross the river at some stepping stones which are quite firm. Over the river bear left to a ladder stile over a wall and then follow the path uphill, first towards a house seen ahead and then bearing left towards the stream to a gate onto a track.

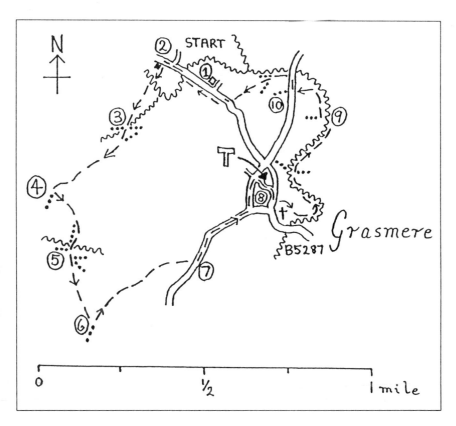

3. Cross the track and go straight ahead across a boggy area to a stile and ahead to a wall to join a clear path. Turn right and continue on this path, soon between walls to a wood kissing gate. The wall on the right now veers away. Continue with the wall on the left until it makes a pronounced left-hand bend.

4. At this point, the main path continues uphill. Do not follow this but take a much smaller path on the left, still by the wall. Grasmere now comes into view ahead. Shortly a wall, broken in places, comes in from the right. Bear right for a few yards to cross this wall and continue in the same direction. The path is very narrow but quite easy to follow as it contours round the hill side. When the path forks take the left branch to emerge at Wray Gill by a wire fence at a very pretty series of small cascades.

5. Cross the beck and continue on the path round the hillside with the wall on the left. 30 yards after Wray Gill there is a ladder stile on the left. It is well worth crossing this and going forward for a few yards to a viewpoint over Grasmere, where there is also a view of the lower cascades of Wray Gill. Return over the wall and continue on a faint path by the wall for about a quarter of a mile to a well-worn path.

Grasmere was carved out by the glaciers and the large central island was formed from debris left behind when the ice melted. It was a favourite excursion of the Wordsworths, who used to row across with a picnic. In his *Guide to the Lakes* he records how he and his sister Dorothy once saw a 'newly created island' in the lake which eventually faded and then turned upside down and disappeared! They decided it was the reflection of Silver Howe in a thin sheet of water over the ice covering the lake at the time.

6. Turn left and follow the path down to the road.

7. Turn left into Grasmere village. Opposite the car park turn left and then turn right to go in front of the Red Lion. Baldry's is a little further on, on the left.

Wordsworth lived in or near Grasmere for most of his adult life and is buried in the churchyard. Grasmere is therefore a place of literary pilgrimage and swarms with visitors. Even without the literary associations it would be a mecca for tourists due to its central position and lovely setting.

Wordsworth was born in Cockermouth in 1770. He went to school in Hawkshead (see Walk 7, page 52) and then Cambridge. On a walking trip with Samuel Taylor Coleridge in 1799, Wordsworth stayed in Church Stile, opposite the churchyard and now the National Trust Information Centre. He found an empty house, Dove Cottage, which he took with his sister Dorothy. In 1802 he married Mary Hutchinson and they had five children.

Dove Cottage was obviously too small so, in 1808, the family moved to Allan Bank, a large house below Helm Crag which Wordsworth had condemned as an eyesore when it was being built. This was not a success and they only stayed two years as Wordsworth was upset by the maintenance costs and smoking chimneys. The family then lived in the rectory but this was cold, damp and melancholy and two of the children died. The final move was in 1813 to Rydal Mount, where Wordsworth enjoyed life as the lynch-pin of the Lakeland intelligentsia and became a national institution. He died in 1850. Dove Cottage and Rydal Mount are open to the public.

The rushbearing ceremony

Two events, the Rushbearing and the Sports, bring even more visitors to Grasmere in August. It was once common practice to cover the earthen floors of churches and other buildings with a layer of rushes. This was warmer and drier than bare earth and every year the rushes were renewed and became a ceremony with a parade and merrymaking in the Red Lion after it was over. Today, rushbearing survives in only a few places, Grasmere being one of them. The ceremony is held on the Saturday nearest to 5th of August, the feast day of St Oswald and the patron saint of the church.

Cumberland-style wrestling is very different from showbiz free-style wrestling and is a serious and skilful sport, even if it is carried out in white singlet and long johns with embroidered swimming trunks on the outside. The wrestling competition which was part of the rushbearing merrymaking became an attraction in its own right and other local sports such as fell running and hound trailing were added. The Sports became detached from the rushbearing, though still held in August, and are now much more famous, attracting thousands of visitors.

Grasmere is also famous for its gingerbread. The Gingerbread Shop was built in 1687 and used as the village schoolroom. Wordsworth taught there for a while. In 1854 it was let to Sarah Nelson who started making the hard and spicy gingerbread, sold to this day.

8. From the tea shop turn left and continue down the road. Just before the church, which is well worth visiting, take the river side path on the left. Follow this by the river until it emerges in a car park.

9. Turn right through the car park and continue through a park on a path by the river and round to the road.

10. Turn right for 100 yards to a public footpath on the left to Butterlip Howe, spelt Butharlyp Howe on the OS map. Follow the main path round the hill, ignoring all smaller side paths, to the road. Turn right, back to the car park.

12. Eskdale and Stanley Ghyll Waterfall

Route:	This is an easy, level, one-way walk along the beautiful bank of the River Esk, visiting a romantic and dramatic waterfall. There are many inviting spots to linger on the river bank so this walk could easily be turned into a leisurely all-day expedition. The return trip is made on the 'Ratty', the narrow gauge railway which runs up Eskdale from Ravenglass. For timetable information, telephone 01229 717171 or there is a timetable at Eskdale Green Station.
Teashop:	Brook House Hotel is open all day throughout the year. It serves both plain and cream teas and a good range of cakes. It has a very pleasant patio outside.
Tel:	019467 23288
Distance:	4 miles
How to get there:	About 2 miles north of Ravenglass, on the A595 Cumbrian coast road, take the minor road signed to Irton, Santon Bridge and Eskdale Green. From the Langdales, Eskdale can also be reached via the Wrynose and Hard Knot passes. Alternatively, the 'Ratty' from Ravenglass stops at Eskdale Green.
Start:	The Green railway station, Eskdale Green. SD 146998

1. Turn right out of the station along the lane. Ignore the road on the left opposite the King George IV and continue on the road signed 'Ulpha and Broughton' over the River Esk.

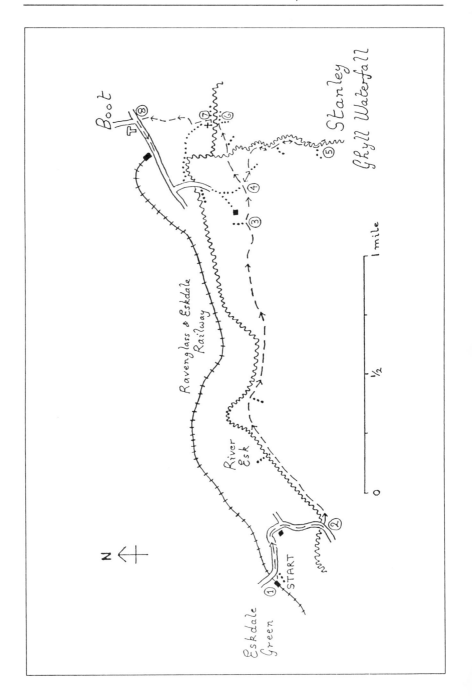

The pub passed on the right is called the King George IV today. Until the First World War it was known as the King of Prussia but hatred of all things German at that time caused its name to be changed.

2. Immediately over the bridge turn left on a public bridleway signed to Upper Eskdale, Boot and Stanley Ghyll by the river and follow this for 1½ miles. The track first follows the river bank and then veers slightly away from it. At two gates take the the path through the one on the right, signed as a bridleway. The path then returns to the river bank before diverging again and going through a lovely wood.

This lovely dale, stretching 13½ miles from the Scafell range to the sea, has everything but a lake. The River Esk rises six miles away by Esk Hause, the 2490 foot crossroads of the fells. It is fed by waters from the east side of the Scafell range before making its way through the more pastoral scenes of Eskdale to the sea. This valley has a long history as a route from the Lakes to the sea. Neolithic stone axes were brought this way from the 'factories' in the central lakes and the Romans improved the road which connected their Galava fort near Ambleside with the port of Glannaventa on the site of Ravenglass (see walk 5) passing Hard Knott or Mediobogdum fort at Hard Knott.

3. Just in front of Dalegarth Hall, which can be recognised by its distinctive round chimneys, the path forks. Take the right branch and follow this to a track.

4. Turn right. After 150 yards go through a gate on the left. The path is signed 'Waterfalls'. Follow the path upstream by a series of footbridges. The best view point is just after the third foot bridge (with a curiously placed stile in the middle) beyond which the path becomes dangerous.

Stanley Ghyll is not the highest waterfall in the Lake District nor does it carry the greatest volume of water, but it is usually reckoned among the finest because of the romantic drama of its setting in the steep-sided gorge. The word 'ghyll' is a romanticised version of 'gill' the Norse word for waterfall. The force with which the water can surge through is demonstrated by the tree trunks in the beck.

5. After admiring the falls, retrace your steps to the track ignoring the path out of the ravine between the third and second footbridges. Turn right to the point where you joined the track and then turn right (*) on a path signed to Boot and Upper Eskdale. Follow the path across the field, over a footbridge and straight ahead to come again to the bank of the Esk.

6. Go through a gate on the left and cross the stream by the stepping stones which are quite solid.

    (Note: This walk can present something of a conflict. The waterfall is obviously most spectacular after heavy rain but then the stepping stones can be less tempting or may be completely under water. In that case at the point marked (*) in instruction 5, above, continue on the track to cross the river at a bridge, ignoring a track on the left leading to Dalegarth Hall. Take a path on the right signed to St Catherine's Church and follow it to the church to rejoin the route at 7.)

7. Follow the track past the church and in 100 yards bear right to the road and the tea shop.

    St Catherine's is the parish Church of Eskdale but is a quarter of a mile from the village of Boot. It was upgraded into the parish church from a chapel of Furness Abbey in the 15th century after the locals petitioned the pope about the difficulty of getting to St Bees for services. The present building is much more recent: The church was more or less rebuilt in 1881.

The font is thought to date from about 1330 and spent sixty years in a farm yard! In 1876, it was recognised and restored to the church. Since baptisms could not be carried out before 1445 when the church was made into the parish church, it must have come from another church.

Tommy Dobson, the bobbin mill worker, who was Master of Eskdale and Ennerdale foxhounds, is buried in the churchyard. His reputation rivalled that of John Peel and when he died in 1910 the memorial was erected by his friends.

The buildings of Boot are on Whillan Beck rather than the River Esk and are up the road next to the tea shop. One of the most interesting is Eskdale Corn Mill which has been restored and is open to the public. There has certainly been a mill here since the 16th century and probably before that.

8. From the tea shop, turn right along the road to catch the train at Dalegarth Station back to the starting point.

In 1872, several veins of high quality iron ore were discovered in the fells above Boot. It was decided to exploit these, despite their remoteness, and a narrow gauge railway was built in 1875 to join the main coastal line at Ravenglass. In 1876 the mine produced 9135 tons of ore. However, the price of ore was falling and the mines soon became uneconomic: mining only lasted eleven years. The railway later carried granite but was never economic and closed in 1913.

In 1915, it was taken over by W.J. Bassett-Lowke who was famous for his model locomotives. He converted it from 36-inch gauge to the even narrower gauge of 15 inches to test his models. The railway also carried goods and services through Eskdale.

When the granite quarries closed in 1953 the railway could not survive on the small tourist trade there was then and closed again. It was eventually bought by a group of enthusiasts, the Ravenglass and Eskdale Preservation Society. It is now one of the most popular tourist attractions in the area. It advertises itself, perhaps without exaggeration, as 'the most beautiful train journey in England'. One of the little steam engines, the River Irt, was built in 1894.

The railway is commonly called 'The Ratty', but no one seems to know quite why. One theory is that it short for Ratcliffe, the name of a man who was closely associated with the original line.

The Ratty

13. Seatoller

Route:	This is a magnificent walk in Borrowdale with superb views of the high fells all around. The return route is a delightful stroll along the bank of the River Derwent where there are many delightful spots to linger and even to take a dip on a hot day (they do happen occasionally in the Lakes!). This is by no means a difficult walk but there is a very short stretch of about 50 yards on the return leg by the river where you have to pick your way over some rocks.
Teashop:	The Yew Tree restaurant is in one of the oldest buildings in Borrowdale dating from at least 1628. It opened as a small cafe in 1954 and today is a well-known restaurant which still serves teas to walkers. There is a pleasant garden at the back. Afternoon tea is served from 2.30 – 5.00pm but it is closed on Friday and Monday.
Tel:	017687 77634
Distance:	6 miles
How to get there:	From Keswick, take the Borrowdale and Honister road. Turn right into Grange-in-Borrowdale.
Start:	In Grange-in-Borrowdale.

In 1209, most of Borrowdale was bought by the mighty Furness Abbey, the second richest Cistercian foundation in England. They owned Derwent Water as well and established the home farm or grange at this convenient position between the two.

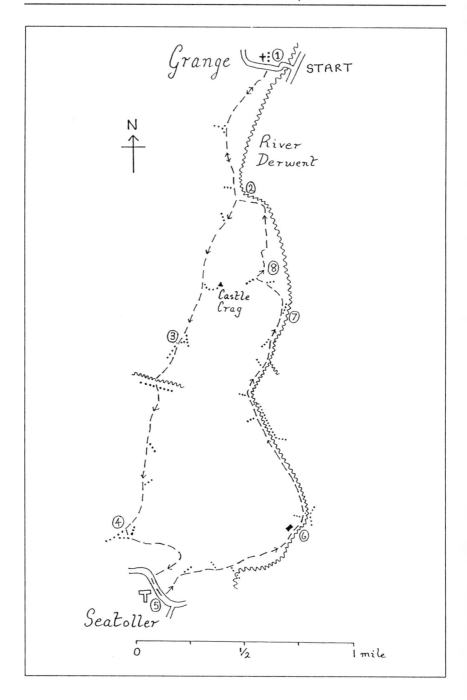

1. Take the public bridleway signed 'Honister Rosthwaite and Sea-toller' almost opposite the church. 100 yards after a gate across the track turn left and follow the track past the campsite to the river.

2. Cross the first stream using the footbridge, ignore a path on the right and then cross a second stream using a footbridge. Now bear right on a public bridleway signed to Seatoller and Honister. This path climbs steadily.

The small but prominent crag to the left is Castle Crag. It can be climbed as a diversion to this walk by those with plenty of energy, a good head for heights and suitable footwear as both the ascent and descent are very steep. The path to the top leaves the main path just before the brow of the hill; descend the same way.

Castle Crag has magnificent views in all directions and is in an excellent position to defend Borrowdale. It is not surprising that it was once crowned by a fort or castle belonging to the Celtic confederation, the Brigantes, which must have been impregnable. In more recent times it has been quarried for slate and sadly, the evidence of this is all around.

Castle Crag is in the care of the National Trust. It was given to them in 1920 in memory of the men of Borrowdale who died in the First World War.

3. Just over the brow of the hill, by a long cairn, take the centre one of three paths. It is signed to Seatoller. Follow this path as it contours round the hill side with magnificent views of Upper Borrowdale in every direction.

Borrowdale stretches from the head of Derwent Water to Seathwaite which, as every school child knows, is the wettest place in England with 131 inches annually though some of the surrounding fells probably have more. Kept well-watered by this abundant rainfall and fertilised by alluvium from the flooding of the river, the flat land in the bottom of the valley is some of the lushest pasture in the Lake District.

Many consider Borrowdale to be the best in this area of outstanding scenery: the lush valley surrounded by towering fells, the woods ablaze with colour in Autumn, the crystal clear river with its deep and mysterious pools and the charming hamlets scattered around. No wonder it is so popular. Without great care and skilful management it could easily be loved to death. It is fortunate that it is mostly in the care of the National Trust.

Dales such as Borrowdale were very isolated in the past and had a reputation for being unsophisticated, to put it mildly. There are many stories told to illustrate this such as the one about the cuckoo wall. The inhabitants of the dale noticed that spring always came with the cuckoos and so they reasoned that if only the cuckoo could be persuaded to stay in the dale, they would enjoy perpetual spring. To this end they build a wall across the valley at Grange to keep the bird in and when the plan failed they decided that they just hadn't built the wall high enough! The local people obviously resented this slur on their intelligence and it is said that if the word 'cuckoo' was said as a Borrowdale man came into a pub, it was enough to start a fight.

4. Eventually the path comes to two small gates within a small walled area. Go through the left-hand gate and down to a track. Turn left and follow the track down to Seatoller. At the road turn left and the tea shop is about 100 yards ahead on the right.

Seatoller developed after 1643 to house quarrymen working in the Honister slate quarries further up the road. In those days the slate was carried by pack ponies round the side of Great Gable to the coast. The quarrymen used to supplement their meagre income by smuggling and the route became known as Moses Trod after a famous smuggler. In the village is the Lake

District National Park Dalehead Base in a converted barn and this has displays and information available.

5. From the tea shop, continue along the road in the same direction for a short distance and then take a public footpath on the left. This starts by the bus stop and goes initially through the car park to a stile by a gate. When the path forks after 25 yards take the lower right fork. Stay on this path as it contours round the hill side and then approaches the River Derwent. There is now the tricky stretch referred to in the introduction but the path very soon improves.

This is Johnny Wood, though it is not clear who Johnny was or what was his connection with this wood. It is a Site of Special Scientific Interest as it is a fine example of oak woodland. The oaks belong to a species typical of the wetter upland areas of England known as sessile oak. In drier regions, the common species is the pedunculate oak. The two species are very similar and you have to look carefully to know which you are looking at. The word 'sessile' means 'without a stalk' and 'pedunculate' means 'with a stalk', so it is rather confusing that sessile oak leaves have a short stalk while the leaves of pedunculate oak have no stalk. The name comes from the acorns and the female flowers from which they develop. In sessile oaks the acorns have no stalk but in pedunculate oaks the stalk bearing the acorns is over an inch long. As well as oaks the wood has a wide range of other trees.

Johnny Wood is also important for its mosses and liverworts which thrive in this damp climate.

6. Pass by Langthwaite Youth Hostel. Do not cross the bridge but continue along the river bank ignoring all paths to the left and right. At one point the 'main' path veers left away from the river for a while, but there is a right of way along the river bank and the main path is shortly rejoined by a stile.

7. Shortly after this the path is forced up and away from the river over a rocky outcrop. Contrary to initial appearance, there isn't a level and easy path along the river bank. After passing through a gap in the wall go ahead on the path passing a cairn up to a T-junction. Turn right.

8. The path now descends to the river again and eventually rejoins the outward route. Retrace your steps back to Grange.

The River Derwent

14. Kings How

Route:	This is a short walk but rather energetic as there is a steep ascent and descent. However, it is worth it for the superb views over Derwent Water and your efforts will be rewarded with a good tea near the end of the walk.
Teashop:	Lakeland Rural Industries is both a craft shop selling a wide selection of items with a lakeland flavour and a teashop. It serves a wide selection of tea time goodies including cakes, scones and flapjacks. There are some tables outside and it is open from 10.00am to 5.30pm in summer and to 4.00pm in winter between March and early December. It is also open over Christmas and New Year.
Tel:	017687 77226
Distance:	3 miles
How to get there:	From Keswick take the Borrowdale road. About half a mile after the turning to Grange, watch for a National Trust car park on the left. This is free to National Trust members.
Start:	Bowderstone car park. NY 253168

1. From the car park, take the path signed to Bowderstone.

The Bowderstone is a glacial erratic: that is, a boulder transported and deposited by a glacier. There are many in this area but the Bowderstone is the best-known because it is so large, easily accessible and apparently perched so precariously.

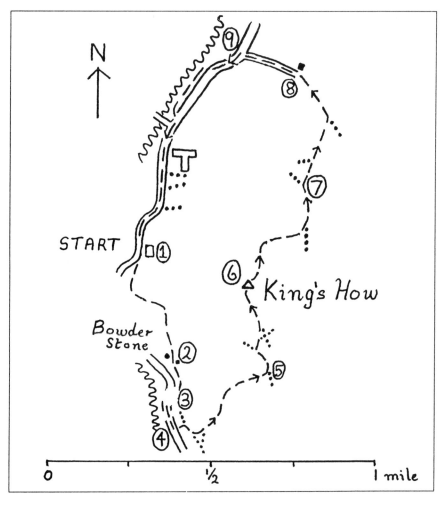

N ↑

START

Bowder
Stone

King's How

0   ½   1 mile

Joseph Pocklington was an eighteenth century showman who
believed in giving visitors to the Lakes something at which to
marvel. For example, he organised mock sea battles on Derwent
Water for the delectation of tourists. He blasted the hole near
the base of the Bowderstone. If you lie down and stick your
hand through, it is possible to shake hands with someone on
the other side. He also built the cottage nearby to house a
guide.

The Bowderstone

2. Continue on the same path to the road.

3. Turn left for 150 yards. There is a path by the river here so it is possible to avoid this short stretch of road walking.

4. Take a public footpath on the left over a stile. After 30 yards, turn right on a clear crossing path. After 150 yards, as you approach a rocky outcrop, take a path on the left and follow it uphill, initially towards a wall, then bearing left so the wall is on the right and eventually up to cross the wall. After crossing the wall continue steeply uphill. The path emerges from the wood and continues climbing through grass and heather to approach a dry stone wall.

Across the valley is Castle Crag – see walk 14.

5. Opposite a gap in the wall turn left and continue uphill, bearing left on the main path and then following it round to the right at the base of a rocky outcrop. Keep heading uphill to the top of King's How, the highest of the rocky outcrops.

Kings How is one of the three summits of Grange Fell. It is small in comparison with some of the other fells round Borrowdale but the view over Derwent Water which bursts upon you as you reach the summit is magnificent, certainly worth the effort of the climb. Wainwright, a connoisseur of fells and views, urges his readers not to neglect this gem despite its modest stature.

Grange Fell and the Borrowdale Birches were bought by the National Trust in 1910 as a memorial to King Edward VII and named Kings How then.

6. From the summit, take the path down on the Derwent Water side and follow it down steeply between rocks and eventually into a wood. Be sure to stay on the main path: there is a maze of small paths around here but the main path is quite obvious and easy to follow. Continue on the same path steeply down through the wood.

7. Watch for a wall starting on the right. Take a path on the right to a stile over the wall. Follow the path down and turn right on a crossing path. Follow the path by a beck through a valley and then bear left, still by the beck, towards some cottages.

This lovely little valley is called Troutdale. It gets its name from the fish hatchery that once was in the beck.

8. Go through the gate and follow the track to the road.

9. Turn left along the road back to the car park, passing the tea shop on the way. There is a footway on the right and it is often possible to walk by the river instead of on the road.

15. Gowbarrow Fell and Aira Force

Route:	This walk combines all the elements that make the Lake District so special. It has woods, a minor summit to conquer, magnificent views of Ullswater and finishes with a visit to one of the Lakes best-known beauty spots – the Aira Force waterfall.
Teashop:	The Aira Force Teashop is a classic teashop which offers a good range of cakes and excellent toasted tea cakes. It has some tables outside which overlook Ullswater. It is open every day from 10.00am to 5.30pm from Easter to November and at weekends in the winter and over Christmas and New Year.
Tel:	017684 82262
Distance:	5 miles
How to get there:	The walk starts at Dockray which is on the A5091 connecting the A66 with the A592. It is about 1 mile from the junction with the A592. There is an area where you can park near the bridge.
Start:	The parking area by the bridge in Dockray. NY 393215

1. Cross the bridge and, in a few yards, take the track on the right opposite the Royal Hotel signed to Aira Force and Ulcat Row. Ignore a path on the left after the last building and continue through a gate in a wall.

2. Turn left on an indistinct path. This reaches a stile in a wall after 90 yards and then continues uphill with a wall on the left. As you

climb, there are superb views backwards (every excuse to stop and admire them) of the foot of Ullswater and High Street. Helvellyn gradually comes into view.

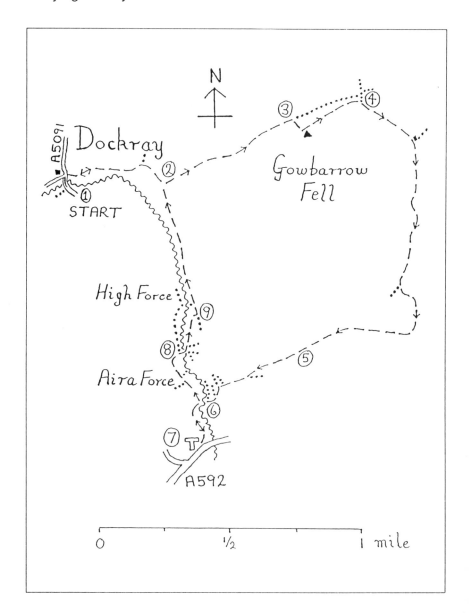

Gowbarrow is often called Gowbarrow Park which refers to the fact that it was a medieval deer park. These were created by the feudal overlords to protect the remaining forest and the hunting. In 1906 Gowbarrow Park, including the famous waterfalls, came on the market as housing plots. The National Trust launched an appeal and £12,000 was raised to buy the 750 acres and save it for the nation.

3. At the highest point of the path by the wall turn right on a clear path and head for the trig point on the summit of Gowbarrow Fell. After admiring the view, leave the summit by the same path. After a few yards, turn right and follow a path downhill to a wall corner seen below and slightly to the left.

   (If you miss this path, which is not very clear to start with, return to the wall and continue beside it to the wall corner and a stile. Turn right to intersect the recommended path.)

4. Just before the wall the path bends right to contour round the hillside and by a derelict shooting lodge joins a path coming in from the left. Continue on this path round the hillside, bearing left at a fork after half a mile. There are magnificent views over Ullswater and there is a seat very well placed to admire them.

   Ullswater is the second largest lake in the Lake District and is 7½ miles long. The geology of the surrounding area is very varied which accounts for its serpentine shape and the variety of scenery surrounding it. The craggy landscape at the head of the lake – the throat of Patterdale – where the steep fells that crowd round the lake are on hard volcanic rock resistant to erosion. In the middle are the softer Skiddaw slates and at the foot is the rolling countryside of sandstone and limestone.

   On the shore of Ullswater beneath Gowbarrow Fell, Dorothy Wordsworth saw the daffodils that were later immortalised by her brother William. She wrote in her diary 'they seemed as if they verily laughed with the wind.'

5. The path gradually descends. When it makes a pronounced right bend to a gate, continue in the same direction for a few yards to a stile over a fence. After 20 yards turn left along a well-constructed path which goes down to a footbridge.

The tower seen below and to the left is Lyulph's Tower. It was built in 1794 as a hunting lodge on the site of an earlier defensive pele tower and is privately owned by the Howard family. Lyulph is said to have come from the name of a Viking called L'Ulf who may also have given his name to Ullswater.

6. Go up the steps on the other side and bear left to the car park. As you enter the car park, take a path on the right which leads to the tea shop.

7. Retrace your steps towards the footbridge. 20 yards before the footbridge turn left and follow the clear path to the lower fall, ignoring paths on the left and right.

The Greystoke family who owned the area in the nineteenth century followed the fashion for romantic landscaping and they planted 60,000 trees of both native and introduced species around the falls and in Gowbarrow Park. This area is called the Pinetum and is a collection of conifers.

8. Cross the river by the footbridge at the top of the fall. Over the bridge, turn left and then bear left along the river bank. Walk along the river bank until the path zigzags up to join another path. Turn left.

Aira Force may not be the highest waterfall in the Lake District or carry the greatest volume of water but it is certainly the best known and is visited by crowds of people every year. This is undoubtedly due to the charm of the falls' setting. It has been a popular beauty spot for over two hundred years and was featured in many eighteenth century guide books used to lead people up to admire the scene. Legends were 'borrowed' to add to the romance. It was said that a crusader met Emma, the daughter of a local lord, by the falls. While he was away she pined and started walking in her sleep. One night he returned and his call woke her. She fell into the torrent and was drowned. The crusader spent the rest of his life, so the story goes, roaming round the falls mourning her and living as a hermit in a cave. Wordsworth used the story and the setting as the theme for his poem 'The Somnabulist'.

9. Continue on this path past the upper falls and through a gate onto the open fell. You soon reach a gate in a wall which you passed through near the start of the walk. From here retrace your steps back to the starting point.

Aira Force

16. Heughscar Hill and Pooley Bridge

Route:	This walk starts by climbing gently through farm land and makes its way nearly to the top of Heughscar Hill. Then such modest efforts as have been made are rewarded as magnificent views across Ullswater come into view. The walk then goes down into Pooley Bridge for tea and returns across pleasant farmland to the starting point.
Teashop:	Appropriately enough, the tea shop is called Heughscar Tea Rooms. It serves a range of delicious cakes as well as cream teas and has a lovely garden leading down to the river. It is open March to November between 10.00am and 5.30pm.
Tel:	017684 86453
Distance:	6 miles
How to get there:	From the B5320 Pooley Bridge to Penrith road 1½ miles north east of Pooley Bridge, take a minor road signed to Barton Church.
Start:	Park by Barton Church. If there isn't any room here, there is a layby on the B5320 not far from the turning. NY 487264

St Michael's church was built in about 1150 and added to over the centuries, especially between 1318 and 1536 when it belonged to Augustinian canons of Wartre Priory, near York. On the north east pillar of the nave is a carved head which is said to be of Edward I or II. Its grand scale shows it once served a

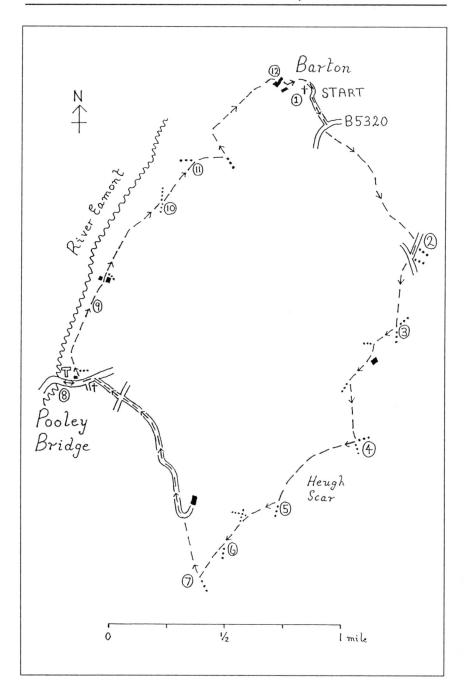

large parish but it was rather superseded by the church in Pooley Bridge which dates from 1868.

In the churchyard are buried Wordsworth's grandfather, Richard, two of his aunts and his grandson. To the left of the path is a sad little gravestone saying 'Tom and Barbara – Orphans of Ullswater': one wonders what unhappy story is behind it.

1. From the church walk to the main road and take a public footpath 5 yards to the right, signed to Celleron. Walk along the left-hand side of two fields. Go over a stile and straight ahead to another stile. Now bear half left to a fence corner and then walk with the fence on the right to a gate and stile onto a lane.

2. Turn right. At the road junction go down the road, signed 'Askam' for 5 yards and then through a gate on the right. Walk along the right-hand side of the field to a stile onto a track.

3. Turn right and follow the track past a farm and through a gate across the track out onto the open fell. Continue on the track to the corner of a walled wood on the left and then bear slightly left for 100 yards to meet an indistinct path marked by a series of cairns.

The town which can be seen behind is Penrith which is a quiet market town now that its traffic problems have been relieved by the M6. Penrith's position on the main route from north to south has given it a turbulent history. It was the object of frequent border raids by the marauding Scots and often razed to the ground. The worst devastation was when 'Black Douglas' fell on the town in 1347. Not only did he and his followers lay the place to waste, they took prisoner every able-bodied survivor.

4. Turn right. This path soon becomes a clear track. Follow it round the hill side as views of Ullswater come into view.

Heughscar Hill is an outcrop of limestone. This rock forms a
broken ring round the Lake District and accounts for the
wonderful springy turf. There are many antiquities in the area
including a stone circle and a Roman road, High Street

5. At a cairn fork right on a path towards a line of trees below. Level
   with the trees, continue round to the left on the main path.

6. When the track forks take the right, lower, fork and follow this down
   to a cross track.

7. Turn right. After passing a farm, the track is surfaced. Follow this
   down into Pooley Bridge, going across a cross roads. At the main
   road turn left into Pooley Bridge. The tea shop is on the right, just
   before the bridge over the river.

Tea by the river

A large pool in the River Eamont gave the name Pooley, a corruption of 'pool by the hill', to the farming and fishing settlement that grew up on the banks of the river. It became Pooley Bridge when a bridge was built across the river in the eighteenth century. Today the pool has disappeared because the river has been dredged and deepened and water is pumped out of the river by an underground pumping station to top up Haweswater reservoir. The bridge still stands giving superb views of Ullswater. Today the village is a popular tourist centre and the starting point for steamer trips on the lake.

8. From the tea shop turn left back into Pooley Bridge. Take a foot path on the left immediately after The Sun. Go through a kissing gate and follow a clear track towards the river.

9. Ascend to a farm and follow a signed footpath past cottages and farm buildings. Go through a gate and follow a clear path across two fields. In the third field, the path is not apparent on the ground but go along the left-hand side of the field, through a gate and immediately through a gap by a stile.

10. After 20 yards go through a kissing gate on the right onto an enclosed path. Turn left and follow the path to a gate. In the next field the path is somewhat less obvious, but follow the fence on the right round to a gate.

11. Go up the right-hand side of the next field to a cross track and a sign post. Turn left, signed to Barton, and follow the track when it bends right, also signed to Barton.

12. At the farm turn right between farm buildings and under an arch. Follow the track round to the left and back to the church.

17. Around Swinside

Route:	This is a charming and easy walk which circumnavigates the small but distinctive hill near Braithwaite called Swinside, which is in view throughout the walk. Most of the route is fairly flat with what climbs there are being short and modest. The teashop is attached to Lingholm Gardens. You can call at the tea room without visiting the gardens but a tour of them is recommended.
Teashop:	The tea shop is attached to Lingholm gardens. It serves a good selection of cakes and has a pleasant covered terrace and garden at the back.
Distance:	4½ miles
How to get there:	From A66 west of Keswick take a minor road signed to Grange, Newlands Portinscale and Lingholm towards Grange. Bear left at two junctions. When the road zigzags take a minor surfaced road on the right which has a sign 'Parking 150 yards'. Park here.
Start:	Parking place at Hawse End. NY 246212

1. Continue along the lane to Skelgill Farm. Go through the gate and continue between farm buildings. At the T-junction turn right and follow the surfaced farm lane down to the road.

Newlands Valley is the setting of one of Beatrix Potter's best loved books. The Tale of Mrs Tiggywinkle tells of an endearing hedgehog washerwoman who lives on the slopes of Catbells, the distinctive hill above and behind at the start of this walk. The book concerns the adventures of a little girl called Lucie with

Mrs Tiggywinkle and is dedicated to 'the real little Lucie of Newlands'.

She was Lucie Carr, the daughter of the vicar of Newlands who really lived at Little Town further up Newlands Valley. The house which is shown as Lucie's however is Skelgill Farm, still recognisable despite some modernisation.

Swinside

2. Turn right for 300 yards to a public footpath on the left beside Newlands Beck signed 'Braithwaite and Portinscale'. Follow the path on the right-hand bank of the beck for about 1 mile, passing an attractive old bridge.

It is difficult to believe now but the Newlands Valley was once the scene of intense mining activity and there are many abandoned mines in the valley. The ore was transported by water to Keswick and smelted using charcoal made from trees

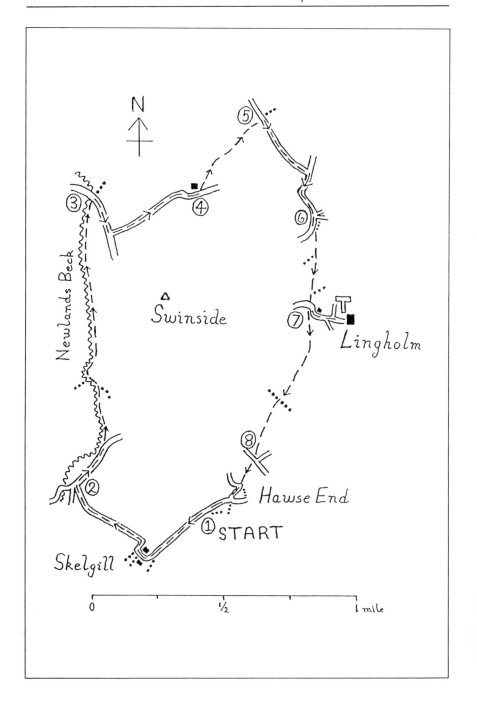

cut from the surrounding hill sides. Copper, lead, graphite and small quantities of silver and gold were all won from these hillsides. Lead mining was still going on in Beatrix Potter's time. She says in her journal for 1885, when she spent a summer holiday in the area gathering material for her books, 'It is a terrible place for drink . . . Every fourth Saturday is the worst, when the miners are paid all their earnings and go to the gin shop.'

3. At the second bridge at a minor road turn right along the road for 300 yards and then turn left signed 'Ullock ^{1}/4 mile'.

4. Just after the last building, Yew Tree Cottage, turn left on a signed footpath through a small gate. Follow the clear path to a lane.

5. Turn right and at the road turn right again.

6. 40 yards after the turning to Nichol End and the entrance to Fawe Park, take a signed footpath on the left. Ignore an immediate branch on the left and follow the path through the wood to a track. Continue in the same direction to the entrance to Lingholm. The tea shop is a short way along the entrance drive on the left, just before the house.

Beatrix Potter and her family spent many holidays in this part of the Lake District. In 1903 the Potters rented Fawe Park for the summer and in several other years between 1885 and 1907 they took Lingholm as a holiday home. During these holidays Beatrix Potter made many studies and sketches which were later used as backgrounds for her stories such as Skelgill Farm referred to above.

Fawe Park is the backdrop to The Tale of Benjamin Bunny and many of the scenes can still be recognised today. However, Fawe Park is not open to the public.

Lingholm is a Victorian mansion built in the 1870s and at the end of the nineteenth century was let as a holiday home. The formal gardens were laid out in the early years of this century when it was bought by Colonel George Kemp who became Lord Rochdale. They are still occupied by the present Lord and Lady Rochdale and the grounds are open to the public. They are well worth visiting, especially in early June when the display of rhododendrons and azaleas is at its best.

7. Return past the lodge to the entrance gate and take a path signed to Catbells next to the gate. Follow the path through woods and across parkland to a road.

8. Cross the road and continue in the same direction on an unsigned path to another road. Turn left and then right back to the starting point.

18. Friars Crag

Route:	This is a very easy walk on excellent paths visiting a classic viewpoint: a determined person could take a wheelchair or pushchair round. For those who think that no walk in the Lakes is complete without some climbing there is a detour up Castlehead, another classic viewpoint, and well worth the effort for the views.
Teashop:	Lakeside Tea Gardens is in a wonderful position overlooking Derwent Water. As its name suggests, it has a very large and attractive garden. It serves a good selection of teatime temptations and is open every day from March until the end of November and at weekends and over Christmas and New Year in the winter.
Tel:	017687 72293
Distance:	3 miles plus half a mile optional detour up Castlehead.
How to get there:	Take the B5289 Borrowdale road from Keswick to Great Wood car park (National Trust) on the left after about a mile.
Start:	Great Wood car park. NY 272214

1. Return towards the car park entrance and, as the entrance road bears left, go through a gate to continue in the same direction through the wood parallel with the road. When the path branches, take the left fork to a track. Turn left to the road.

2. Turn left for 50 yards to a gap in the wall on the right. Turn right on the path, back the way you have come, and follow this path for about three-quarters of a mile.

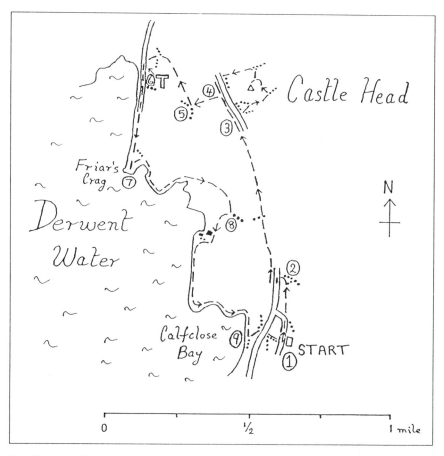

3. To visit Castlehead

a) Go through a gap in the hedge on the right 20 yards past the 30mph sign.

b) Cross the road and go over a stone stile into a wood.

c) Follow the main path uphill ignoring side paths to the left and right.

d) As the path levels and approaches the boundary wall, take a smaller path steeply uphill on the left. This is opposite a fenced gap in the boundary wall. Follow this to the summit, joining another path just below the summit.

At the summit is a welcome seat and a plaque illustrating the view. Castlehead has long been one of the classic excursions from Keswick and the view is far better than that from many, much higher, peaks.

The summit of Castlehead is one of the best places to appreciate the effect of geology on scenery. To the north and west are the more easily eroded Skiddaw slates and they have produced the rounded outlines of Skiddaw itself, Grisedale Pike, Causey Pike and the distinctive Catbells in the foreground just across the lake. Contrast this with the precipitous crags and rugged outlines of Walla and Falcons Crags and the Jaws of Borrowdale shaped from the resistant lavas of the Borrowdale Volcanic rocks. It is the effect of the weather on the various rock types which gives the variety of Lake District scenery.

Castlehead itself is the vent of one of the ancient volcanos and it is the remains of the lava which once plugged the vent, too hard to be completely eroded by the glaciers.

Derwent Water was created by the action of ice. The basin was carved out by glaciers and then blocked by a terminal moraine, or pile of debris, left when the glacier melted. At that time there was one large lake but this has been separated into Derwent Water and Bassenthwaite by eroded material being washed down from the fells above. Derwent Water itself is being gradually filled in this way. At the south end is a marshy area which is steadily encroaching on the lake.

e) Leave the summit the same way initially. Do not take the path you came up by but continue straight down to a cross path at the edge of the wood.

f) Turn left to the road.

g) Cross the road to the path and turn left to rejoin the main route at point 4.

A view of Derwentwater from Castlehead

4. Take a footpath on the left signed to the Lake.

5. On entering the wood turn right on a crossing path and follow this to emerge in the car park by the Century Theatre. Cross the car park and turn left on the road for a few yards to the tea gardens.

6. From the tea gardens, turn left past the jetties and along the lake shore. When the surfaced track ends, continue in the same direction to the tip of Friars Crag.

Friars Crag is a deservedly popular view point over the Queen of English Lakes and into the Jaws of Borrowdale. It is much photographed and painted and it will certainly not be quiet!

Derwent Water has four islands each with its own history. The one nearest to Friars Crag is Derwent Isle. Derwent Isle was once owned by the German miners who came in the sixteenth century to win copper, silver and lead from the surrounding fells.

They used it as a vegetable garden and brewery. In the eighteenth century it was bought by the showman Joseph Pocklington. He built a series of follies including a mock druid's circle based on nearby Castlerigg and used it to stage mock sea battles.

South of Derwent Isle is Lord's Island and south of that is Rampsholme Island. Lord's Island was the seat of the Earls of Derwent Water, the last one of whom was beheaded for supporting the 1715 Jacobite rebellion. Legend tells us that the young wife of the last Earl escaped from the island and made her way up the steep gully of Lady's Rake on Walla Crag to go to London with the family jewels to plead for her husband's life. Though it is historically true that she did make every effort to save him the family had in fact left their island home many years before, after the Civil War.

Furthest away from Friars Crag is St Herbert's Isle. This is named after the seventh century hermit who lived there and it is said that pilgrim's embarked at Friars Crag when making a pilgrimage to his shrine and from this Friars Crag gets its name. More prosaically, it was probably used by the monks of Furness Abbey when visiting their property in Borrowdale as in those days of poor roads, the lake was used as a highway.

Friar's Crag is made of the same rock, dolerite, that makes up Castlehead and is a dyke or wall-like intrusion into the slate. It was probably once a feeder to the volcano which once covered this area and has since been almost completely eroded away. It was purchesed by the National Trust in 1922 as a memorial to Canon Rawnsley who was one of the founders of the National Trust. There is also a memorial to John Ruskin.

7. After admiring the view, continue along the lake shore and then follow the path away from the shore into a wood.

8. Leave the wood and turn right on a cross track and follow this past the entrance to a house. As the track approaches a cottage, bear left on a signed footpath and follow this round the lake shore into Calf Close Bay.

9. In the middle of the bay, follow the path left away from the shore and up towards the road. Just before the road bear right to a gap in the wall and cross the road to another gap. Take the left-hand one of three paths to the car park.

19. Bassenthwaite

Route:	This is one of the longest walks in this book so plenty of time should be allowed for it. It is not particularly arduous, however, and can be enjoyed by all except the most committed couch potato. It visits every sort of landscape the Lake District has to offer — fells and fields, woods and water and even a bit of bog so be prepared! Bassenthwaite Lake is in view for most of the walk. One of the highlights of this walk is the stretch along the shore of the lake. When the lake is very full this path is flooded and becomes impassable. It is then necessary to follow a diversion.
Teashop:	The Old Sawmill Tearoom is, not surprisingly, in an old sawmill building and is decorated with old tools. It serves a good range of cakes and other teatime goodies and has some tables outside. It is open from 10.30am till 5.30pm from mid March through to the end of October.
Tel:	017687 72287
Distance:	8 miles
How to get there:	Bassenthwaite village is signed from the A591 Keswick to Carlisle road.
Start:	The village green in Bassenthwaite village. NY 230322

Bassenthwaite village is somewhat off the beaten track though its pub, the Castle Inn, is popular. The church, St Bega's, is about 3 miles from the village, and this suggests that the focus of the settlement has shifted down the centuries. This interesting old church will be visited later in the walk.

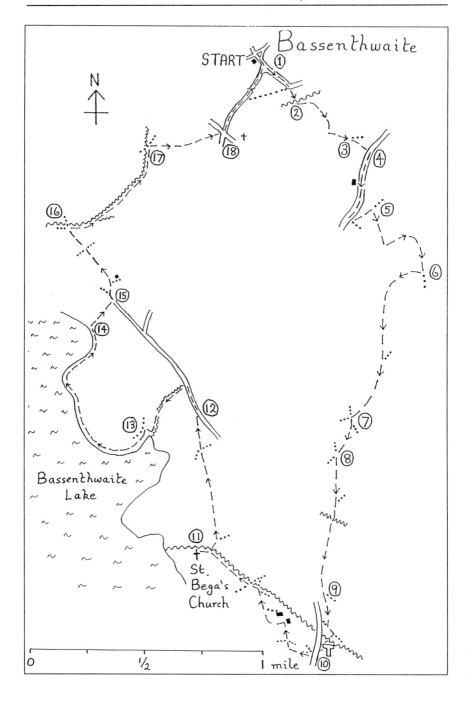

1. From the village green walk to the large barn at one end and turn left. After about 50 yards take a minor road on the left to continue in the same direction. When the lane bends left continue in the same direction over a stone stile.

2. Cross Chapel Beck by a wooden footbridge and turn left. The path shortly bears right away from the beck up to a stile. Continue ahead along the left-hand side of the field to cross another stile. Now follow the fence round to the right to yet another stile. Go across the field but do not go through the gate at the far side. Instead turn left and walk with the fence on the right.

3. Watch for a bridge-cum-stile by a tree in the fence on the right. Cross this and bear half left to a stile on to a lane.

4. Turn right. 300 yards after the entrance to High Side House turn left on a track, ignoring a path on the right after 20 yards.

5. When the track fades away turn right to keep a gappy row of hawthorns on the left. 150 yards after the hawthorns end, at a point marked by a post with an arrow on it, turn left to a stile by a gate. Cross the field to a second stile by a gate and follow the initially faint track curving right.

The mountain looming ahead (which we are not going to climb on this walk!) is Skiddaw. It is formed of Skiddaw slate, an ancient and more easily eroded rock than the volcanic outpourings that formed the crags of Borrowdale, not that far away. This has produced the somewhat more rounded shapes of these fells. Despite its height, it is quite an easy mountain to climb and thousands make it to the top every year: all you need is plenty of puff and perseverance though some would say that the climb is rather boring.

In the last century, Skiddaw was home to a Scotsman, George Smith. He was something of a recluse and lived in a hermitage he built himself on the slopes of Skiddaw Dodd. He was a good

portrait painter and swopped his pictures for whisky. This was
his undoing, sadly, as he became an alcoholic and was in
constant trouble with the authorities.

6. Go through a gate across the track and immediately turn right
uphill by a wall. Walk with the wall on the right and continue in the
same direction when the wall finishes and a conifer plantation
begins. Ignore a path on the left and follow the same path steeply
downhill to a gate into the plantation.

This is Dodd Wood. Originally, all the lower slopes of the fells
would have been covered in native broad-leaved forest but over
the centuries this was cleared leaving bare hillside. Thomas
Storey of Mirehouse was a pioneer of reafforestation and began
planting Dodd in 1790. The very large conifers which will be seen
later near the tea shop are remnants of planting in the early
nineteenth century.

Dodd Wood is now leased from Mirehouse by the Forestry
Commission. In the 1920s the emphasis was on rapid replanting
to replace the trees felled in the First World War and create a
national reserve of timber. No attention was paid to the impact
reafforestation can have on the landscape. Conifers were
planted in blocks of different species with hard, unsympathetic
edges and vertical firebreaks that were scars on the landscape.
In more recent times, the Forestry Commission has changed its
attitude and pays more attention to the effect on the
landscape of its work. It is working to a long term plan to blend
the forest more naturally into the landscape.

The value of forests for recreation has also been realised and
this one has been opened up to the public. The owner is as keen
as the Forestry Commission to encourage public access and
many waymarked walks have been devised.

7. Go through the gate and after 30 yards turn left on a wider path that descends gently to a cross path.

8. Turn left and follow this path for about half a mile.

9. Take the right fork down to a surfaced forestry track. Turn left and after 65 yards turn right on a footpath down to the teashop.

Mirehouse dates from the seventeenth century, with later additions, and is in a magnificent position on the shores of Bassenthwaite Lake with Skiddaw behind. The house reached its greatest fame in the last century when it was owned by two hospitable brothers, James and Thomas Spedding and was visited by many intellectual giants of the day. Thomas Carlyle, a regular visitor, wrote of his 'kind friend who lives sheltered about the rock of Skiddaw'. Sir Charles Lyall, an authority on fossils who was a major influence on Charles Darwin, and the painter John Constable were also visitors.

Another frequent guest was also Alfred Lord Tennyson who once apparently sold his Chancellor's Gold Medal for English Verse for £15, so that he could pay for a trip to Mirehouse. He drew much of the inspiration for the description of King Arthur's last hours in the *Idylls of the King*, carried off across the lake in a barge rowed by ghostly figures with three queens wearing golden crowns, from the setting by the shore of Bassenthwaite Lake.

Mirehouse is still owned by the Spedding family and is now open to the public from April to October on Sunday, Wednesday and Bank Holiday Monday. Tickets can be bought at the tea shop. The house contains numerous mementoes and portraits of the Spedding brothers and their distinguished guests.

10. Turn left along the road for 50 yards and then take a public footpath on the right through a gate. This soon joins a track to continue in the same direction. Turn left in front of some buildings and then

take the first track on the left to a gate. Through the gate, cross a track and follow a public footpath in the same direction to St Bega's church.

St Bega's church

The church is dedicated to St Bega and dates back to at least the tenth century. Its circular churchyard suggests that the church may have replaced a pre-Christian religious site. It was heavily restored by the Victorians but still retains many Norman features. A guide book can be purchased inside which gives a wealth of detail. St Bega was the daughter of a seventh century Irish chieftain and she is supposed to have fled from her father's court on the day she was to marry a Norse prince. She landed in England at St Bees on the Cumbrian coast. Legend has it that she was transported there by angels. At St Bees she founded a convent which in later centuries became large and powerful. She was bothered once more by her rejected suitor and she sought refuge with the King of Northumbria and helped to found the Abbey at Whitby. Today she is rather obscure but this was not always so. In the window recess by the pulpit is a copy and translation of a hymn to St Bega from a fifteenth century *Book of Hours* in the Bodleian library.

11. From the church, retrace your steps for about 50 yards and then turn left on a track. After about 100 yards, as the track bears right, bear left to a stile into a small wood. Follow this path through the wood, across a field, through a second small wood and across two more fields. The path is not visible on the ground in the fields but goes straight ahead from gate to gate. Cross a track and continue across one more field heading towards the right-hand side of a wood, to a stile onto a lane.

12. Turn left. Just before a bridge over a stream turn left over a stile and follow the path by the stream. At a wire fence go over a stile on the right.

(Note: if Bassenthwaite lake is very full continue along this quiet lane to rejoin the recommended route at the point marked '*' in instruction 14, below)

13. Turn immediately left to the lake shore and follow an, at times, indistinct path over a series of stiles along the lake shore.

Bassenthwaite Lake is the most northerly of the lakes and one of the largest but is less well known than some of the others. It was once joined to Derwent Water forming a much larger lake: the two became separated by the deposition of eroded rock from the surrounding hillsides forming an area of low lying land between them.

The lake is owned by the National Park. It originally belonged to the Egremont Estates but they made over the lake and some of the surrounding land in 1979 in settlement of estate duties. Use is restricted to protect the environment and wild life. There are no power boats and sailing is restricted to Royal Yachting Association members who can use the facilities of Bassenthwiate Sailing Club on the other side of the lake.

14. 10 yards after a gate into a very narrow strip of woodland, turn right on a path up to the lane. (This is where the diversion from the point marked '*' in instruction 12, above, rejoins the main route.)

15. Turn left and after 100 yards bear right up the surfaced drive to Scarness Farm. When the drive bends right up to the house, continue in the same direction on a grassy path to a gate. Through the gate bear half right down the field to another gate. Now continue ahead by picking your way across an area which is boggy except after extreme drought to a kissing gate.

16. Do not cross the bridge but turn immediately right along the bank of the river. Cross it at the next bridge, just after its confluence with another river and continue in the same direction. Over a stile, the path is less clear but continues with the river on the left through one field and three-quarters of the way along the second.

17. Watch for a stile on the left onto a track. DO NOT CROSS THIS. At this point, turn right across the field to a small gate. Go across the fields from stile to stile and then bear slightly left to a gate to a cross roads.

18. Take the lane opposite back to Bassenthwaite village.

20. *Hesket Newmarket and Caldbeck*

30/12/98
with Edward

Route: This is a very easy and attractive walk between two interesting Cumbrian villages. It is in part of the National Park undeservedly overlooked by many visitors and so is very quiet compared with the rest of the Lakes.

Teashop: The Watermill Restaurant in Priest's Mill at Caldbeck is open every day in the summer from 10.00am to 5.00pm extending to 7.00pm on Tuesday to Saturday in June, July and August. From October to December it is closed on Monday and it is closed entirely in January and the first half of February. Priest's Mill is an old water mill used as a corn mill from 1702 until 1933. After that it was a sawmill and joiner's workshop until 1965 when floods destroyed the mill dam. The award winning restoration was completed in 1986 and the building now houses a restaurant serving excellent afternoon teas, as well as craft workshops, a gift shop and an fascinating museum of Lakeland mineral mines. There is a small garden which overlooks a cricket pitch.

Tel: 01697 478267

Distance: 5 miles

How to get there: From the A66 Penrith to Keswick road 8 miles east of Keswick take a minor road signed 'Mungrisdale and Caldbeck' and follow the signs to Caldbeck until you reach Hesket Newmarket.

Start: Car park at east end of Hesket Newmarket. 342386

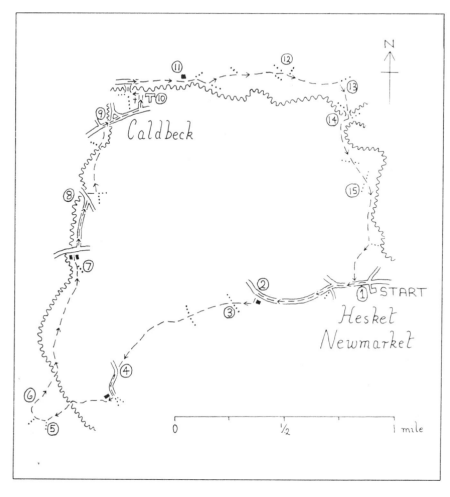

Hesket Newmarket's market was new when its charter was granted in 1751. Today it is an attractive village centred round a wide street and village green with many 18th century buildings. On the village green is the market cross and, next to it, the bull ring, still there after 200 years. Charles Dickens stayed here with Wilkie Collins and wrote about it in *The Lazy Tour of Two Idle Apprentices* published in Household Words in 1857.

The owners of the Old Crown Inn converted a derelict barn at the back of the pub into Hesket Newmarket's brewery in 1987. They produced their first beer – Blencathra bitter – in 1988 which won the best bitter award at the CAMRA (Campaign for Real Ale) festival in 1989. The brewery now produces five beers which are also available in several local pubs as well as the Old Crown.

1. From the car park turn left through the village. When the main road bends right by the Temperance Hall, continue straight ahead on a lane for ½ mile.

2. At Street Head Farm turn left on a track signed public footpath and follow it through two gates, bearing right.

3. Continue ahead at a cross path as the track leaves its enclosing wall and fence and becomes a footpath, not readily apparent on the ground at the time of writing. Bear slightly left to a stile and over the stile the path is enclosed again, this time between fences. Cross a surfaced track and continue on the track ahead for just under ½ mile to a lane.

4. Turn left. When the surfaced lane ends at a complex junction of tracks, turn right on a track signed public footpath. Follow it round behind buildings. Cross a stream and after about 250 yards watch for a stile by a gate on the right where the track bends sharply left.

5. Cross the stile and follow an indistinct path downhill next to a wall on the left. After a while, the path becomes more obvious and continues with a wire fence on the left. Ignore the first stile on the left. Cross the second stile on the left and continue in the same direction, now with the fence on the right.

6. When the fence on the right ends, the path is not at all clear on the ground. It contours round the bottom of the hill, bearing left. At the start of a dry stone wall continue ahead towards a depression to the right of some light coloured boulders. Cross a stream by a concrete bridge and turn left to a gate. Go through a second gate ahead after 10 yards and then walk along the left hand side of two

fields. Continue in the same direction across a third field towards a large silo.

7. Join a track and follow it between farm buildings to a road. Turn right for 25 yards then left on a lane signed 'Upton and Caldbeck'.

8. Immediately before the road crosses a beck, take a signed footpath on the right along a track. After 90 yards, as a stone wall starts on the left, turn left over a stone stile. Follow the path along the left hand side of a field to a stile and then down through trees to a footbridge over a beck. Continue on the obvious path, ignoring a stile on the left, to a road.

9. Turn right through the village. Just past the church turn left along a track signed to Priest's Mill to the tea shop by the river.

Priest's Mill at Caldbeck

Caldbeck is named after the river – the Cold Beck – on which it stands. The first building was probably a hospice for travellers built by the monks from the priory at Carlisle. The church was started in 1142 and dedicated to St. Kentigern who was also known as St. Mungo. He came from Scotland to preach Christianity in the 6th century and there are other churches dedicated to him in the Lakes, such as the one at Crosthwaite on the edge of Keswick. Behind the church on the river bank is St. Mungo's well.

Caldbeck's two famous residents are buried in the churchyard. John Peel, the famous huntsman, was born in Caldbeck in 1776 though he spent most of his life about six miles away at Ruthwaite. The song which immortalised him was written by his friend, John Woodcock Graves, after a day's hunting in 1832. It became nationally famous after William Metcalfe, the choir master of Carlisle cathedral, set it to the tune we know today. John Peel died after a hunting accident at Ruthwaite in 1854.

The other famous resident is Mary Robinson, the daughter of the landlord of the Fish Inn in Buttermere, who must have been very appealing because she was known as the Beauty of Buttermere. A new and wealthy resident in the district, the Hon. Augustus Hope M.P. for Linlithgow, was attracted to her and they were married on October 2, 1802. Shortly after the honeymoon he was arrested. The marriage had been mentioned by Samuel Taylor Coleridge who was a correspondent for the Morning Post. Charles Hope, the Earl of Hopetown, was surprised to hear of the wedding when he knew his brother was on holiday in Europe! The bridegroom was found to be one James Hatfield, a confidence trickster with another wife and a trail of swindled victims.

He escaped and evaded arrest for two months. He was not charged with bigamy but with defrauding the Post Office as he had been franking his own letters. The jury at Carlisle were reluctant hang a man for fiddling the Post Office but were stirred by the fate of Mary, by then pregnant, and her predecessor. John Hatfield was hanged on September 3, 1803.

The case caught the public imagination and several books and plays were written about the events surrounding the Beauty of Buttermere. It does not seem to have done Mary much harm. She returned to her father's inn where she became quite a tourist attraction. She eventually married a farmer from near Caldbeck and lived a long life, raising a large family before she was finally laid to rest in the church yard.

Caldbeck was an important industrial centre. Priest's Mill was just one of several mills powered by Cold Beck and its tributaries. In addition, the fells above Caldbeck were rich in minerals. Mining began in the 13th century and continued until the 1960s.

10. After tea go down to the river and turn left on a path between the church and the river to a bridge over the river. Cross the river and turn right along a track.

11. When the track ends at the entrance to the water works, continue ahead on a path to the right of the buildings and then bear right through a gate. Follow the path through the woods bearing left uphill after about 150 yards. Ignore a track joining on the left and when the path forks, bear left up to a cross path.

12. Turn right and follow the path until it leaves the wood at a small gate. After this the path is not apparent on the ground but continue across the field in the same direction for 100 yards until you are level with a stile in the fence on the right.

The wide view from this spot is one of the highlights of the walk. The wind generators which can be seen on the hills lie outside the National Park – they would not be allowed within it.

13. Turn right to the stile and cross it. Over the stile the path is indistinct. It lies slightly to the left down through trees and gorse, straight across an open area, down through a patch of scrub and then across a field to a bridge over the river at a small, attractive gorge.

14. Over the river bear right to a stile and then round to the left to a small gate and on through a wood. When the wood peters out, follow the path shown by yellow arrows. This crosses a rutted track and bears slightly right along the side of a small valley to a gate, crossing another track.

15. Follow the path through a wood to a wooden kissing gate by a metal field gate. Go through the wooden gate and follow the clear path to Hesket Newmarket and the start.

Fact sheet - Keep in touch!

Thank you for buying this Sigma Leisure book.

We hope you enjoy the walks (and the teashops!) but if you have any comments or suggestions, we want to hear from you. Please use this tear-out sheet to tell us about any problems you encounter, so that we can investigate them and make this book even better. If you can't fault the book, tell us that as well!

Bear in mind that footpaths are sometimes diverted, new teashops appear and, very occasionally, opening hours might change. Very, very rarely, a teashop closes for good so that we have to make major changes to the book. You can see how useful your experiences are to us in making a better product.

Your name & address: ....

....

....

Comments:

(continue overleaf if necessary)

IN SEARCH OF SWALLOWS & AMAZONS:
Arthur Ransome's Lakeland

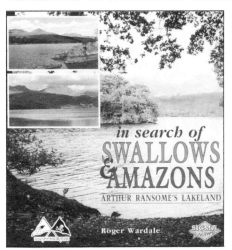

– Roger Wardale

This is a new edition of a popular book originally published in 1986. Additional material has been added to satisfy even the
most avid reader of "Swallows & Amazons"
– three decades of Ransome hunting with
text and photographs to identify the loca-
tions of the ever-popular series of books.
There's a two fold pleasure in this book –
enjoying the original stories and discover-
ing the farms, rivers, islands, towns and
hills that formed their backdrop.

This book is an insight into a uniquely English author, a celebration of Lakeland scenery and a good read in its own right. £6.95

WALKING LAKELAND TRACKWAYS:
the Eastern Lakes

Mike Cresswell

This is the companion volume to Mike
Cresswell's "Walking Peakland Trackways".
The walks enable the reader to discover
the historical significance of the paths,
tracks and minor roads that crisscross
the Lake District. They include: Roman
Roads such as High Street and Kirkstone
Pass; Mediaeval and Trade Routes – the
Corpse Road across Wasdale Head and
the Drovers' Road at Muncaster; Turn-
pikes – from Shap to Kendal and Ambleside to Grasmere. In all, 24 well-planned
routes that bring history vividly to life.
Distances range from 6 to 16 miles. £7.95

THE LAKELAND SUMMITS: a survey of the fells of the Lake District National Park

Tim Synge

"A really workmanlike job"
MANCHESTER EVENING NEWS

£7.95

FULL DAYS ON THE LAKELAND FELLS: 25 challenging walks in the Lake District

Adrian Dixon

£7.95

STROLLING WITH STEAM: Walks along the Keswick Railway

Jan Darrall

£4.95

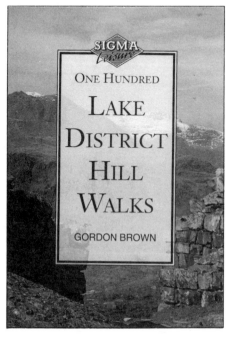

100 LAKE DISTRICT HILL WALKS

Gordon Brown

"A useful addition to any walker's library" WEST CUMBERLAND GAZETTE.

£7.95

LAKELAND WALKING: on the level

Norman Buckley

"A good spread of walks" RAMBLING TODAY.

£6.95

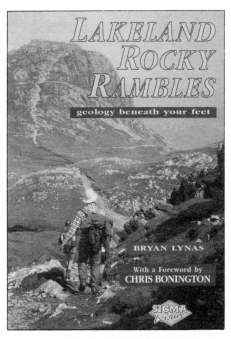

MOSTLY DOWNHILL: Leisurely Walks in the Lake District

Alan Pears

"Perfect companion; thoroughly recommended" MENCAP NEWS.

£6.95

LAKELAND ROCKY RAMBLES: Geology beneath your feet

Bryan Lynas

Foreword by Chris Bonington

This is the companion book to Snowdonia Rocky Rambles: the perfect way to learn about why things look the way they do.

"Refreshing ... Ambitious ... Informative ... Inspiring" NEW SCIENTIST.

£9.95

PUB WALKS IN THE LAKE DISTRICT

Neil Coates

£6.95

CYCLING IN THE LAKE DISTRICT

John Wood

£7.95

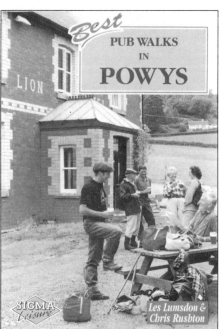